Epstein   Take Me to Your Chalet

Cover design and illustrations by Hans Kuechler

"It is severely forbidden to pass through the meadows before finishing the haymaking by a fine of frs. 10.–."

– Sign in an Alpine meadow

Eugene V. Epstein

Take Me to Your Chalet

Further Tales of Life in Switzerland
By the Author of

Once upon an Alp

and

Lend Me Your Alphorn

Benteli

For Sooth and for Bear

© 1982 by Benteli Publishers Berne
Layout and printing by Benteli Inc., Berne
Printed in Switzerland

ISBN 3-7165-0411-4

Contents

- Snow Job 7
- Very Important Parson 17
- Water, Water, Everywhere 25
- Loveli Lili 31
- Family Friend 35
- Hard Work 47
- Beverage Leverage 61
- Dial L for Landlady 65
- Dialectics 73
- Choo-Choo Train 85
- The Swiss Slalom 89
- Mock My Words 97
- Life Can Be Fine 107
- Talking of Walking 115
- What's in a Name? 125
- Horse Sense 135
- The Last of the Wurst 147

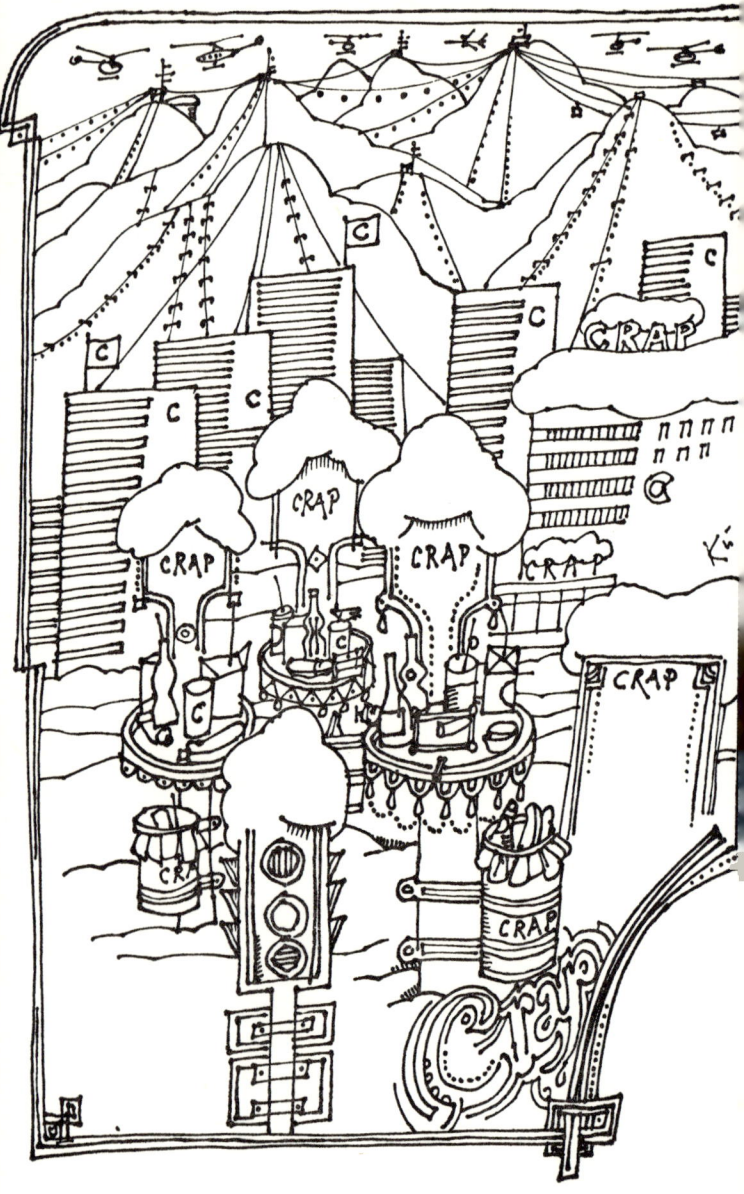

Snow Job

My proficiency on skis is legendary throughout Switzerland. I might modestly add that I have also written numerous scientific papers on the subject of skiing, most of which are available from friendly neighborhood booksellers on all nine continents. One of my studies, "Compatible Gravitational Considerations in the Design and Construction of Ski Slopes", has long been accepted as the definitive work in its field and has directly led to the construction of dozens of new ski areas in Switzerland alone.

At the moment, the development of ski areas is limited by local construction and environmental laws, mainly because of such things as trees, streams and similar impediments. Fortunately for the thousands of skiers who look towards Switzerland as the mecca of their sport, the skiing and ski-lift lobbies have joined forces under the name CRAP (Confédération romande et allemande de pistes) to assure that anyone who wants to ski in Switzerland can find the slope of his heart's desire. It is particularly fitting that CRAP is also the Romansh word for "stone" – a word all of us hope will soon capture the imagination of skiers everywhere.

Franco Domizil, newly elected president of CRAP International, attempted to explain the aims and desires of the new organization in his inaugural address:

"Ladies and gentlemen, the purpose of CRAP is to extend the life expectorancy of every man, woman, boy, girl and child through Good Health. Good Health, as we all know, means SACRIFICE, and Sacrifice is what we're here for today. Ladies and gentlemen, CRAP is our answer to those of the left who accuse us of destroying – yes, I said *destroying* – their beloved landscapes. In the first place, I ask you, how can a landscape be destroyed? A landscape can only be improved. Improved for everyone, not only for the generally unwashed few who just want to look at it, but improved for the vast majority of hard-working and upstanding citizens – those who believe in our 3 M way of life: monotony, monogamy and monopoly.

"At the moment, ladies and gentlemen, there are barely enough ski areas in Switzerland to satisfy the needs of our own people – not to mention theirs. In addition, despite the heart-warming progress made in highway-construction, a lot still needs to be done. Did you know, for example, that Switzerland's highway system is extremely limited when compared to those of other skiing nations, such as the United States of America, which alone has innumerable highway-miles more than Switzerland?

"My suggestion, ladies and gentlemen, is that Switzerland should begin calculating in miles instead of crummy old-fashioned kilometers. Imagine how terrible it sounds if we say we have 5000 kilometers of new highways, turnpikes, parkways and turnkeys. Just think of what elemental progress could be made if we were allowed to say 3106.8497475 miles instead of 5000 kilometers – how simple our lives would be! The opponents of CRAP would be left ... they already are, of course ... the enemies of CRAP would be bereft of theft, they would soon forget that we ever measured kilometers in kilometers and would begin to think in terms of miles only. And so, my very dear friends, we come to Point No. 1 of our overall program: *Kill Kilometers and Put the Mile Back in Style!*"

The applause was deafening as Franco Domizil reached his climax and announced to all and sundry:

"This may be Monday, all and Sundry, but we CRAPPERS want to thank you for your kind deprecation, for which we shall be forever cacophonic. Actually, your hearty applause should be addressed to our Director of Corpulent Communications, Montague Merde, who personally created our wonderful and incredimental slogan. As we always say in the office, 'It takes a fast gun to think up a slow-gun.'

"Now, ladies and gentlemen, let me conclude, before turning over the floor and walls and ceiling for general discussion, by explaining why CRAP is so important to us. And why we need new roads to enable skiers to reach their destinations with as few delays as possible. As you all know, skiers love snow. No one realizes this more than I, for I am constantly involved with the stuff. In fact, my work has been characterized as a pure snow job. Yet, to be honest with you, what earthly good is snow if you can't get to it? Oh, maybe there are still a few old-fashioned painters still alive who think white is pretty. Every schoolchild knows that! But you've got to get up to the snow in order to enjoy it – and it's our job to spread the word throughout Switzerland: no roads, no tourists; no tourists, no skiers; no skiers, no stock of skis; no Stokowskis, no conductors; no conductors, no trains; no trains – no roads! We need m-o-r-e, I say! More highways mean more of the good life!"

More applause. For who, if anyone, would turn down the "good life" in favor of the "bad"? No one, that's who. And no one did, as Franco Domizil concluded his remarks and turned over the meeting for questions from the floor.

The first question came from Hermann Haut, Managing Director of Consolidated Bratwurst

Ltd., and one of the heavy industry representatives present at today's meeting.

"Dr. Domizil, I first want to thank you for all that dreck – uh, all that information – about CRAP. We at Consolidated Bratwurst stand ready to assist you in any way we can, especially if we can sell more sausages to the skiing public – but that is obviously not our main interest. But here's my question: I would be interested to know how large an area would be taken up by ski slopes if all of them were rolled into one. Are you in a position to provide such information?"

"Yes, I am, as a matter of fact. First of all, you realize that such a thing would never happen – I mean, how could you roll all those slopes into one large slope? Not unless we managed to rent an entire canton – say, the Canton of Graubünden – which we're actually trying to do – and turn it into nothing else but a gigantic *piste*. We're well on the way already, you know, for, if you are a reasonably good skier, you can ski all over the place for as long as fourteen days without ever leaving the prepared slopes. Our goal is to increase this figure to sixteen days and to add thirty-nine new aerial cableways, forty-nine new chairlifts, fifty-nine forklifts and sixty-nine facelifts. In this way, we hope to conquer all those forces of Man and Nature who are against us: Man with his kinky environmental nonsense, Nature with her (she is a she, isn't he?) attempts to foul up our efforts with avalanches and so on. Well, we've engaged the Army to shoot down any avalanche that dares to make a move, and we think we'll soon have the problem licked. To come back to your question, Mr. Haut, the ski slopes of Switzerland comprise a total area at the present time about equal to the Canton of Zug.

"I realize that you might possibly be shocked by this information. Please remember, however, that Zug is the very smallest of our Cantons, somewhat like Rhode Island would be to the United States. So I'm sure you will consider our goal of three to four cantons to be quite reasonable. After all, what difference would it make – we've already got so many cantons and even one new one, the Canton of Jura, the home of so many jurists. Our wish is to establish the Canton of Crap as the home of so many crappy skiers. In this new canton nothing will happen that is not in one way or another connected with the Skiing Industry – excuse me, I meant to say the Skiing Sport.

"Think of the miles of sausages which would be consumed on our slopes, think of the mustard, the bread, the paper plates! Ah! It makes my heart go pitter as well as patter and my stomach rumble! I see a beautiful day in the mountains, highways, of course, leading to every restaurant and chalet along the way. Gorgeous sunshine, cerulean sky, Nature at her finest and all that, plus perfect snow, touched up here and there by the latest in snow-making machinery. Charming, rustic chalet-type skyscrapers with chain restaurants for heavy smokers, fast-food emporiums for the gourmet, a vast selection of hamburgers with or hamburgers without, hamburgers to take or hamburgers to not.

"Is this a dream, is my fantasy running away with me? Think of the cars, the sales of sports equipment, the bars, the grills, the all-night dancing – and all because of me and my CRAP! Do you begin to get the picture, do you begin, now, to see why we need your cooperation? We need more than money – although, quite francly, we'll take all we can get. But we need to start an educational process – right from the primary-school level. Teach the dumb bastards – uh, sorry, our schoolchildren – that CRAP is good for them, that they will grow up to be better adulterers because they have learned what's important and what isn't in life. And the sooner they realize this, the better off we'll all be. The most important lesson is simply that CRAP is important!"

The roar was again deafening, reminding those present that the verdict was virtually unanimous, a true sign of democracy in Switzerland. "One moment, please – one moment, I'd like to say something, if you all don't mind." The voice came from the rear of the auditorium. "My name is Bandwurm, Dr. Alexander R. Bandwurm. The R. stands for Ragtime, my mother's maiden name. I'm an orthopedic surgeon and, like the rest of us, I'm here today and gone tomorrow. I mean, I'm here representing the Confederation of Swiss doctors, hospitals, health insurance companies and you name it – I've forgotten most of the others. Anyway, I simply wanted to draw your humble attention to the fact that there are more broken arms and legs in Switzerland than we can shake a crutch at. Although we are, in a way, happy that we can provide high-quality medical attention to the injured, we wonder if this will still be the case in the future. After all, more highways, more skiers, more broken arms and legs, more hospitals and more doctors needed all around. What's the feeling on this subject? Is it really so healthy when you break so many bones? Do we really need all that CRAP stands for?"

Franco Domizil at first looked somewhat embarrassed at this apparently unexpected question. Then he began to turn purple, visibly losing his composure. Like so many people who lose their composure, he no longer knew what the score was. Angrily, he shot back at Dr. Bandwurm:

"Listen, My Good Doctor! I'll make a suggestion to you. Stop holding back progress, you hear! Stop bringing up details like broken arms and legs or maybe we'll have to start thinking of broken craniums while we're at it. For whatever happens, just remember, will you, that CRAP as an institution is here to stay. The more CRAP today, the more everything will come out all right in the end!"

THE END

Very Important Parson

The expressions one learns in foreign-language courses can be quite ridiculous. For example, I have been waiting for thirteen years to use the Swiss-German sentence I memorized so carefully and practiced so often:

"*Grüezi, fröiläin, wändzi zum pfaarer syner husheltteri?*" (Good evening, miss, I understand that you would like to visit the parson's housekeeper?) One day, while rehearsing this pithy Swiss expression in front of the bathroom mirror, my friend Walti appeared out of nowhere. I didn't notice him until I had reached "... zum pfaarer syner hushelteri" for the thirty-fourth time, totally exhausted and gasping for breath.

"What in the name of Horatio are you doing – going into show business or something?" Walti always began our conversations by trying to irritate me. But I always remain cool.

"Quatschkopf!" I screamed. "What do you mean, what am I doing? What do you *think* I am doing? Don't you ever think before you look – I mean, talk? For your information, Walti, I am reciting the Swiss-German phrase I am supposed to learn for next week's class. Swiss-German, Walti – a language of which I believe you must have heard, particularly since you were ostensibly born here."

"Oh, so that's it ... Swiss-German? I see," said Walti. "Must be some dialect I don't know. But, all right, Eugene, whatever you're speaking – and we can discuss that in a moment – why are you speaking it in front of that mirror? Are you a masochist or something?"

"No, I'm not, damn it all! I admit that I would rather look at *my* face than yours – if that indeed is your face that you keep wagging at me! Quite simply, old buddy, I am speaking Swiss – and all I wish to do at the moment is to guide a young lady to the parson's housekeeper. Instead of criticizing, you could also volunteer to help me, *oder?*"

"No, I'm definitely not the parson you're looking for – ha-ha-he! Eugene, I never knew that you go to church on Sundays ... so that's what you've been up to? Ruthli and I always thought you were out with your ..."

"Shut up immediately, Walti! Or I shall be forced to ask Ruthli how good your Italian grammar is. Let's see, now. How many years have you been going to Italian classes on Tuesday evenings? Twenty ... or only eighteen? I've forgotten. Gosh, you must be really good, fella!"

"Okay, okay, I think we understand each other, *caro mio*. But returning to your thoughtful question, my Italian is not as bad as you seem to think. The last phrase *we* learned was 'honor among thieves'. Now Eugene, I hope I don't have to keep reminding you ... *l'onore sotto ladri* ... capisce?"

"Me capeesh tutti. As a matter of fact, Waltero, me capeeshe tutti frutti ... how you lika dat, keed?"

"I merely wanted to stop by on my way home to ask how you are," replied Walti. "Thanks for your kind reception, but, really, please don't put yourself out for me. I'd hate to impose, you know!"

"All right, all right, stop with the self-pity. I promise not to put myself out, but thanks for reminding me about the cat."

"The cat?"

"Yeah, the cat. Thanks for reminding me to put the cat out ..."

"You're impossible!"

"*You're* impossible! *Gatto nero!*"

"Let's stop this now!"

"Roger, let's stop this now!"

"Who's Roger?"

"God! Are you ignorant!"

"Are we stopping?"

"I have, but you haven't," I told him.

"What do you want ... the Treaty of Versailles in six copies?"

"There you go again with your foreign languages, Walti! I'm trying to learn your peculiar language because I strongly believe in getting to know the natives and all that tommyrot. I'm trying to be a nice guy, don't you understand how difficult that is for me?"

"You mean being a nice guy is difficult, or getting to know our delightful tongue?"

"Now you just reminded me of something else besides the cat: the most delightful Swiss tongue I ever ate was with you."

"You ever *ate?*"

"Yeah, you remember the night – years ago – when you and Ruthli introduced me to my first *Metzgete?* The tongue was incredibly good! Smoked, I think."

"No, it was salted ... good, though, you're right. But I preferred the blood sausage. That's what I like!"

"Aha! Caught in the act! Now I've got you, Waltilein! Who's the masochist ... me with my mirror on the wall or you with your bloody sausage in the Fall?"

"Listen, Eugene," Walti interjected. "Can't we please stop this infernal scrapping and get down to business?"

"Sure we can, only what business were you thinking of today, Honorable Swiss Friend No. 1? Monkey or dirty?"

"I shall choose to ignore your last remark, Eugene. I'd like to help you with the housekeeper and her boyfriend if you wish me to. Now where were we?"

"Not her boyfriend – the parson! She's the parson's housekeeper, remember?"

"Why should one thing rule out another?"

"Walti, we're not discussing the parson's love life – or anyone else's for that matter!"

"Then why are you bringing him girls?"

"Bringing him ... what?"

"Bringing girls to the parson ... you said so yourself. When I came in you distinctly mentioned guiding a young lady to the parson's house ..."

"... parson's house*keeper*!"

"Then who is the girl and why are you with her? She's probably jealous because of the housekeeper's liaison with the parson and wants to get rid of her ... just like on Swiss TV."

"Yeah, just like Swiss TV ... and you make me just as sleepy, too! When I want a soporific, I'll ask for one, okay?"

"Sure thing. But how did we get onto the subject of sloporifics, anyway? I only offered my help so that you can properly address the young lady you are so avidly trying to impress."

"Trying," I repeated impatiently, "to address a fictitious, nonexistent, feminine figment of my imagination in order to improve my skilfulness with your tongue and hers."

"Leave my tongue out of this, Eugene! I suppose she can decide what she wants to do with hers!"

"Walti, one more chance ... then *basta!* I said she was a feminine figment ..."

"I thought you said '*pig*ment'!"

"How could I have? ... I haven't seen her yet! Oh, blast it! Would you stick to the subject – just for once, Walti? Please ... pretty please with sugar and cyanide?"

"That's what I've been trying to do all along, Eugene. Let me recapitulate: first there was no girl, then she was a figment – she doesn't exist – then she exists enough to help you with her tongue. Isn't that what you said?"

"Walti, you are unique, you know that? I've never met anybody, anywhere, who so constantly thinks of the same thing ... you have a one-track mind, you know that?"

"One-track ... yes, of course ... monorail ... our firm is presently working on plans for a revolutionary monorail system for the next Swiss National Exposition."

"Please, Walti! I can't take it anymore! We have known each other for a brief eighteen years, but couldn't you make an exception? Couldn't you forget your Swiss rules of etiquette and treat me as a friend – even if we haven't known each other for fifty-five years? Come on, friend, help

me with my Swiss-German, will you! Please?"
"Of course! That's what friends are for. Now what is it you wanted to say?"
"I would appreciate your assisting me with my pronunciation and enunciation in connection with the following phrase: '*Grüezi, fröiläin, wändzi zum pfaarer syner hushelteri?*'"
Walti just sat there shaking his head from side to side. "Eugene," he said, "I honestly wouldn't know where to begin ... it sounds so grotesque when you speak our language! Even more than it does normally. Eugene, do we really have to deal with this parson and his housekeeper?"
"Yes, we do. And I have to learn all about them by next Wednesday. Or is somebody missing the point?"
"If somebody is, you ought to call the police."
"The ... police?"
"Yes ... and ask for the bureau of missing parsons!"

Water, Water, Everywhere

I had just arrived in Vulpera, determined, for one of the few times in my life, to do something tangible for my health. I was impressed by the name "Vulpera" – to me it had a singularly romantic ring – and in addition I had never before visited the Lower Engadine Valley.

But my health, of course, was the real reason. My good friend Eddie, always ready with a word of advice, told me I looked terrible. My wife, obviously out of salutary considerations, was not particularly displeased when I announced one day to all and sundry: "Believe it or not, dear Family, I shall be leaving tomorrow – into the wilds of the Engadine Valley, where I intend to take the waters, both in me and around me!"

"Have a great time!" they wished me in chorus. "And don't come back too soon!"

I approached this experience with a certain degree of trepidation. The most important reason, of course, was that I had no idea what kind of water I was supposed to drink, gargle or swim in. Where I come from, water was something wet that came out of a faucet and with which half the population occasionally washed – and that was that. And, furthermore, there was only *one* kind of water. If anyone had thought of naming water faucets after saints, famous doctors or movie stars, he would have been declared hysterical and sent to a purgatory of boiling, steaming mineral geysers.

And now I suddenly found myself in the pump-room, or water-drinking hall, near Vulpera, lurking suspiciously in a corner – in my usual shy and self-effacing manner – wondering what I was supposed to do next.

"Good morning, young man. Are you here in our lovely pump-room to take the health-giving waters?" I looked towards the lady who had addressed me.

"Yes," I replied. "What do I do next?" She gazed at me sympathetically and, with a voice like that of a nurse before a major operation, asked what was wrong with me.

"Wrong with me? Well ... er ... ah – I don't really know how to answer your question. I'm actually feeling fine. It's just that Eddie and my wife, you know, they thought I ought to do something for my health."

"And right they were!" she shot back. "Whoever they are! Now stop stalling and tell me what's wrong with you. Have you, for example, had any recent maladies of the liver or bile ducts, such as inflammation of the gall bladder, gallstones, congestion, insufficiency, cirrhosis and toxic damage of the liver or after-effects of tropical diseases? Well, have you?"

"Heavens, no!" I answered. "My God, do I look like *that* sort of person?"

"Then," she continued, "how about your digestive system, particularly your gastric motility? Or have you ever had nervous dyspepsia?"

My face reddened, for questions of an intimate nature always tend to embarrass me. "Excuse me," I said, "but I really didn't come here to talk about my private gastric system – or even yours, for that matter. I just wanted to have a plain and simple glass of water."

"Not so fast, young man!" she replied. "How about your circulatory system ... your urinary system ... your ..."

I had to interrupt. "That's it!" I exclaimed. "My one and only urinary system! My world-famous urinary system!" And I added, with obvious pride, that I had once had a small kidney stone. The lady now seemed to dance for joy. She was, in any case, totally carried away by my admission.

"You see!" she said. "I knew that you couldn't be *that* healthy! Even handsome, sporty, desirable men like you just always have *something* wrong with them – and it's my job to find out what it is."

The kind lady kissed me approvingly on both cheeks, with tears of joy dripping profusely from the tip of her prodigious nose. "Young man," she said. "Bonifazius and you were made for each other. Drink the curative waters of the Bonifazius spring and thou shalt forever go forth healthier – and in any case wetter." After telling me that she always drinks this particular water herself, she burped discreetly and pointed reverentially towards the faucet labelled 'Bonifazius'.

"But wait!" I said, looking more carefully at the various faucets around me. "Why may I not try Luzius or, perchance, his sisters Emerita and Carola? I've heard that they are also extremely good, especially for what ails you."

"Of course they're good, but not for you. At least not until you develop something wrong with one of your other systems. Right now, you're clearly a urinary-tract case, so take this glass and drink a toast of pleasure at the spring of Bonifazius – the Benefactor."

"Yeah, sure," I countered, "and I even know Benny's brother Max – we went to different schools together! I also happen to have noticed that Luzius has quite a bit more sodium and potassium – not to mention old-fashioned gas – than Bonifazius, while Emerita is absolutely loaded with calcium and strontium – at least compared to Carola. But you're right," I added. "Bonifazius looks superb in the fluoride, chloride, bromide and sulfate departments. As a matter of fact, I've never seen such a well-balanced, well-proportioned spring in my whole life. I'm sure that Bonifazius will do my mixed-up insides a world of good!"

The kind lady smiled understandingly now. Then she sent me off to drink my Bonifazius.

I drank the 335 grams of Bonifazius water she prescribed for me and, apart from the rather revolting taste, I began to feel better almost instantly, especially as Bonifazius went through me like a rocket on the First of August, the Swiss National Holiday. "You know," I said to the lady after having recovered my composure, "you were so completely right. I feel the good health and happiness welling up inside me! I'm sure that Bonifazius and I – despite his questionable taste and gaseous content – will certainly become the very best of friends." I then said goodbye to the sweet lady who had just changed my life. And, as I left the pump-room, I burped as discreetly as I could.

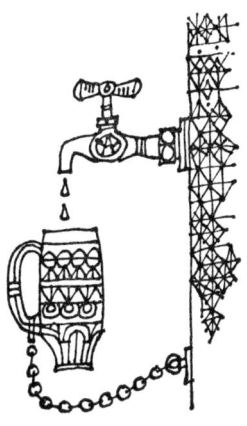

Loveli Lili

The Swiss-German language, if I may politely use that designation, abounds in its wonderfully imaginative use of the diminutive. Of course, if one thinks about it, this is not an entirely surprising state of affairs, considering the size of the country. Basically, everything is considered small in Switzerland – even if it is large. For example, it is not unusual for the Swiss to speak of a "grosses Fäschtli" (a little large party), the "li" ending indicating that whatever was once of moderate size has now been reduced to proportions more easily understood by the average citizen.

But there is yet another group of words in Swiss-German which rarely seem to appear in other languages, and collectively represent an important aspect of living in this country. Here I refer to the intimate and congenial type of words which reflect a certain familiarity with the subject being discussed. For instance, a Swiss would hardly ever say "Gymnasium" when referring to a higher-level school. No, his word is "Gymi", much like "Uni" for university and "Handeli" for Handelsschule (commercial school), which, you will possibly notice, also happens to include the ominous "li" ending.

There are *li*terally thousands of such words, and

no one – as far as I know – has ever bothered to make a *li*st of them. Having no particular subject which interested me at the time, I began to collect some of these unique terms in the hope of contributing something more to posterity than I have heretofore.

Imagine for a moment that you are a member of the *Pfadi* and that an old lady asks you to buy something in the *Molki* for her *Znüni*. You think to yourself, "Ha! I would much rather go to the *Badi* and drink a *Coggi* or spend my time reading the *Tagi* or a *Krimi* in the beautiful Swiss sunshine."

But no, the little old lady insists that boys are in the *Pfadi* for precisely such purposes as helping little, as well as big, old ladies. So off you go to the *Molki* to purchase some *Yogi* and *Gomfi*.

When you finally appear at the little old lady's home, she invites you in for some *Znüni*, but you politely decline with the excuse that you haven't yet done your *Uufzgi*. Anyway, she says "Merci vielmals" to you and offers you a bar of *Schoggi* which you, in turn, are forced to refuse because your *Zahni* has warned you what *Zucki* can do to your molars and bicuspids. You then decide to drive your *Töffli* to the *Badi* after all, and, as you speed off, you regret that no one took a *Foti* of your good deed for the day.

Did everyone understand this touching Stori? If

not, allow me to offer an unofficial translationli of what actually happened. In the first place, you are a member of the boy scouts (Pfadfinder = *Pfadi*) and a lady asks you to buy her some provisions at the local milk store (Molkerei = *Molki*) for her morning snack (*Znüni*, or that which is eaten at nine o'clock). You would apparently prefer to visit the local beach (Badeanstalt = *Badi*) and drink a Coca-Cola (*Coggi*) or spend your time reading the Zurich newspaper *Tages-Anzeiger* (*Tagi*) or a detective story (Kriminalroman = *Krimi*) in the incomparable Swiss sunshine.

But wait! Our Swiss lady reminds you that you are a boy scout and she eventually convinces you to rush off to the *Molki* (remember?) for some yoghurt (*Yogi*) and jam (Konfitüre = *Gomfi*).

When you return to her home, the lady invites you to join her for some *Znüni*, but you refuse on the pretext that you haven't yet done your homework (Aufgaben = *Uufzgi*). She therefore bids you adieu and offers you a bar of chocolate (*Schoggi*), which you then refuse because your dentist (Zahnarzt = *Zahni*) has cautioned you not to eat sugar (Zucker = *Zucki*) because it might adversely affect your toothlis. You finally ride off on your motorbike (*Töffli:* don't ask me why) to the beach and, as you drive off, you sincerely regret that no one took a photograph (*Foti*) of you know who doing you know what. Well, that's enough for today. Love*li li*ttle Lili with the *li*mpid eyes, one of my numerous and more *li*beral ladyfriends, is coming over for a small *li*bation. Mere fantasy, you say? Then ask me no questions and I'll tell you no *li's!*

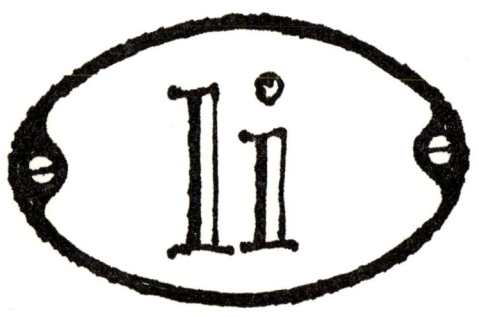

Family Friend

Certain moments in our lives can be particularly meaningful to us. They are perishable moments, deceptive experiences we try to recapture but cannot. Stubbornly we hold on to fleeting and shadowy memories, cherishing them, re-living them – yet all too aware of our helpless inability to turn back the clock. This is the stuff of which Nostalgia is made; it occurs when age and experience conspire against those who were once naive and innocent – and perhaps, to some extent, still are.

Frank was a special friend of ours, a family acquaintance long before I personally appeared on the scene. He was a German-born architect who came to New York a good quarter-century before I was born – and he was already close to twenty years old.

Frank met my parents somewhere, somehow, through a mutual friend, or who knows how – the way those things tend to happen in life. It developed into a close friendship, despite some conspicuous differences in background and culture. My father was born in White Russia, near Minsk, my mother came from New York City. Frank had been living and working in New York for some ten years when my father first arrived in the United States. Allow me at this

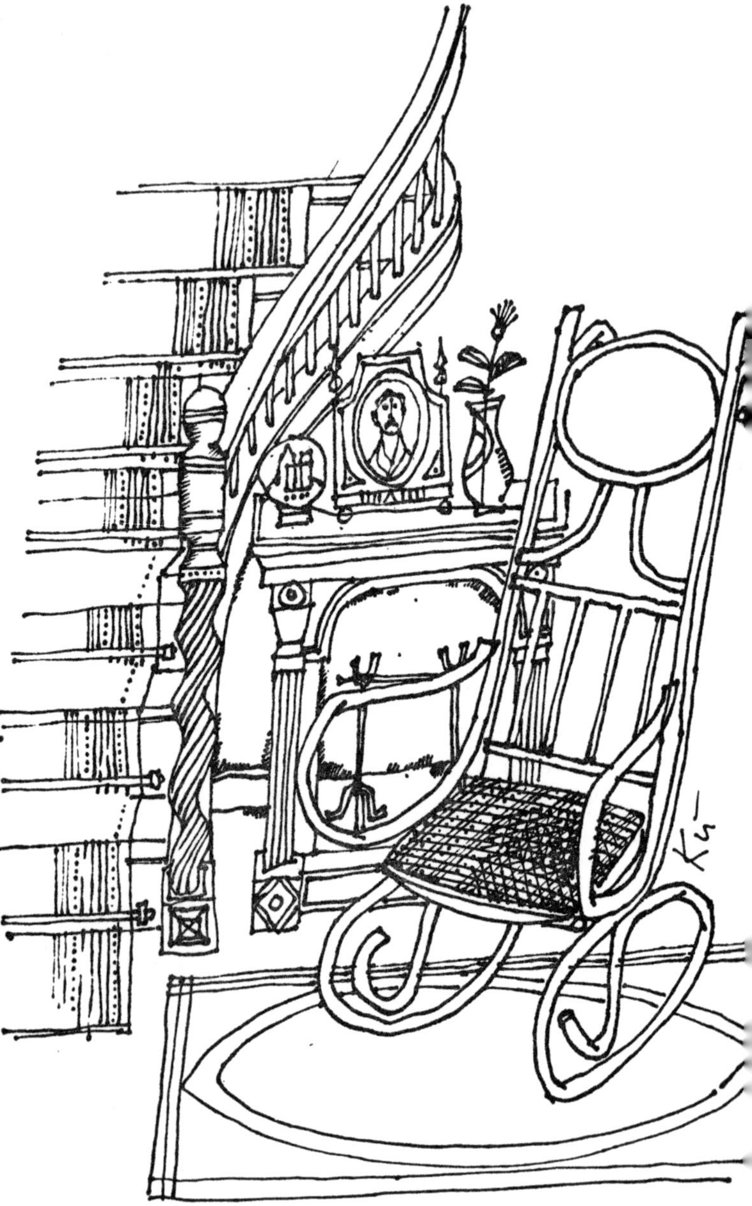

point to assist the confused reader. I don't know when they met, my parents and Frank the architect, but I do know that they were quite close, for Frank, from my earliest memory, seemed to be a permanent fixture at our house and in our lives.

I blinked at the bright world for the first time when Frank was forty-five – this is the point I wanted to stress. Let us assume that I first became aware of the man when I was four or five: he would then have been fifty. As I grew up, he was always somewhere nearby. I recall that he lived at many different addresses, all of them in our little town on Long Island. I doubt that we ever visited Frank's home more than three or four times – and I never knew the exact reasons why. According to my mother, Frank had "certain" problems at home.

Frank often lived in houses he himself designed. They all had a special "German" look, according to remarks I must have overheard. I also often overheard my parents with Frank and a couple from Scotland when they met on Saturday evenings at our house to talk mainly about William Shakespeare. The Scotsman was an eminent Shakespeare expert – a member of the prestigious Shakespeare Club of New York. We thought he knew everything there was to know, and very possibly he did. These evenings were invariable: once at our house, once at the home of the Shakespeare expert, just down the street. The program was also invariable: lighted fire in the fireplace, a lively discussion based on a few quotations from *Richard III* or *A Winter's Tale*, coupled with digressions into any subject that seemed interesting – fishing, sailing, Franklin Delano Roosevelt – and an invariable intermission. At this point my mother brought in English tea and a heaping tray of salmon-salad sandwiches. Mind you, not smoked salmon – merely mashed-up salmon from a tin, mixed with mayonnaise and a few other condiments, plus a slice of lettuce. In America, a sandwich wasn't a sandwich without lettuce in it.

My place in this congenial configuration was not *in* the room but *above* it – halfway above it to be precise. I sat out of sight – or so I thought – on the staircase, behind the railing or whatever it's properly called. I must have been very small and almost invisible in those days, although I honestly don't recall when those days were. Let's say they were between my fifth and tenth year on this earth.

I think my parents knew about my staircase-listening habits. Perhaps they thought that such early intellectual exposure might eventually have a salubrious effect on the sluggish mind of their younger son and obvious genius. Please don't think me totally devoid of humility, not to mention modesty.

The Saturday night discussions in which I had never taken an active part were more or less as I have described them. As the reader must now be aware, my ability to digress is incomparable: it could only have been learned from experts. I also learned – without realizing it – that there are nuances and accents in life which can assume entirely different meanings when looked at in the light of specific events. Salmon-salad sandwiches are a good example for me. Even today I cannot eat them without unconsciously thinking of Saturday nights and Shakespeare. There are too many aspects of those evenings to be aired here – except to note that television did not yet exist. But conversation did.

Towards the end of a typical Shakespeare evening, the Scotsman generally fell asleep in his chair for a few moments and was left in peace. When he awoke, he continued to participate in the discussion without missing a beat.

I shall now digress back to Frank, having fulfilled my purpose: to "place" him in my life and in his times. As I mentioned earlier, the presence of Frank was taken for granted by all of us. What I did not mention was his unusual background in history, language, European culture and, of course, architecture.

Please note that I have mentioned "European culture" for the first time, and it at once becomes our signal to leap boldly into the future – from Saturday evenings round (and above) the fire to my own very first taste of the Old World itself.

Now *I* was twenty and playing the same game backwards. I was travelling to Europe! Frank had come to the United States at the beginning of the century at about the same age as I was now. He had often talked of his early experiences in New York. I particularly remember his stories about five-cent lunches in Lower Manhattan, their having included an enormous glass of beer and as much as one could eat of innumerable tasty dishes laid out on the bar. Well, they *sounded* tasty anyway.

Frank also told bedtime stories to me and my brother, more often than not about the legendary and very Teutonic Black Forest, where he, incidentally, didn't come from. He invented names for wizards, fairies, hobgoblins and gnomes, names that sounded very German, very ominous and very foreign. And witches were known throughout the Forest for a particularly mystical imprecation – "honeybumbumgüldigunderberg!" – which Frank loved to repeat and repeat. In any case, we considered ourselves extremely lucky to have been born in America, for terrible things always seemed to be happening elsewhere but never to us – everyone knew that.

I arrived in Zurich shortly before my twenty-first birthday. Frank was also in Europe, also in Switzerland, living with one of his sisters in Malans.

That's all I knew about the place: its name. Malans. I recall that it sounded fresh and crisp. Malans. I distinctly remember a particular letter to my parents I wrote at that time; in it I singled out names of Swiss towns and villages which I considered to be particularly resonant or euphonious. Arth-Goldau at the foot of the Rigi, for instance. I wrote two or three pages on Arth-Goldau – why I don't know, for I had never been there. Perhaps I thought of golden art or I don't know what else. But Arth-Goldau became symbolic for me, for in that letter I had tried to explain a "feeling" that had apparently overcome me: names sounded different, they were also pretty names, but unlike the prettiness of Munsey Park, Westbury, Roslyn, Sand's Point. Had I subconsciously, as well as physically, left the Anglo-Saxon-sounding world of my youth?

So Frank was in Malans and I was living in Frau Böschli's *Pension* on Gloriastrasse in Zurich, learning for the first time in my life that I had to pay for every bath I took (two francs fifty). The wall telephone we were allowed to use for outside calls was virtually the centerpiece of Frau Böschli's boarding-house: it was placed in the precise geographical center of the corridor between the living- and dining-rooms. This was no doubt a practical solution, for everyone could hear the phone when it rang and no one had to run too far to answer it. It also meant, of course, that everyone could hear everyone else's conversations. Were these kind people – my first human contact with the Old World – so interested in the lives of others? Let us ignore this unthinkable possibility for the moment – for this is neither the time nor place for such twiddledaddle. Nor are my faithful readers likely to put up with much more digression in this story, which – I cross my heart and hope to die! – is now about to begin.

Frau Böschli was always aware of who was telephoning whom, while a little meter rang up the exact cost of each call and made a horrible buzzing sound when the call was finished. Frau Böschli would then waddle madly into the corridor from the kitchen, usually with a potato in one hand and a paring knife in the other. She would straighten her glasses on her generous nose and squint at the telephone meter, which was still buzzing – an inadequate word to describe the stridency of that din. To me it sounded rather like an electric chair someone forgot to turn off. Frau Böschli would then push a special button and the infernal gadget stopped protesting. She then carefully wrote down the amount of the call – not including a basic charge of twenty centimes, which she never forgot – and the name of the guest responsible. In retrospect, this scene became clear to me: there was a reason why that wall telephone was in the geographical center of our *Pension*. Hearing, running and paying. No mistake about that! Based on what I later learned about Switzerland and the Swiss, the phone was probably at the geographical center of Zurich as well, not to mention the Universe. When the Swiss are accurate, they are very, very accurate indeed.

Our wall telephone rang one day during breakfast. It was for me, my first call ever in Europe. The civil engineer, who was often at our breakfast table, answered. He beckoned me to the phone, mumbling something about a friend of mine in Graubünden who wanted to speak to me.

Graubünden? I couldn't possibly have pronounced Graubünden at that time, nor did I, for that matter, have any idea whom I knew in such an unpronounceable place.

It was, of course, Frank. He was settled in Malans, he said, and I ought to come down sometime – it was beautiful there and the grapes were ripening. And we could take walks high into the mountains. He said something about "Heidi country" but I didn't discover the significance of this expression until years later. (To an American, I suppose, all of Switzerland was Heidi country. Frank meant a specific area – Maienfeld–Jenins–Malans – where the stories ostensibly took place.)

Completely disregarding the Heidi element, Frank und I agreed to meet in Sargans and to walk to Liechtenstein! I hung up the receiver, the buzzer buzzed and Frau Böschli waddled and skipped out of the kitchen to check the meter. No charge. After all, Frank had called *me*.

Liechtenstein! Now I remembered. Of course! Years earlier, Frank had given me a complete set of Liechtenstein stamps for one of my birthdays. Liechtenstein was famous among stamp collectors. Bright, colorful stamps in odd shapes and sizes, portraying princes, princesses and castles. Only the witches were missing.

But now Liechtenstein really existed for me – and not in the Black Forest, either, but within walking distance of Sargans. Wherever that was.

(To be continued)

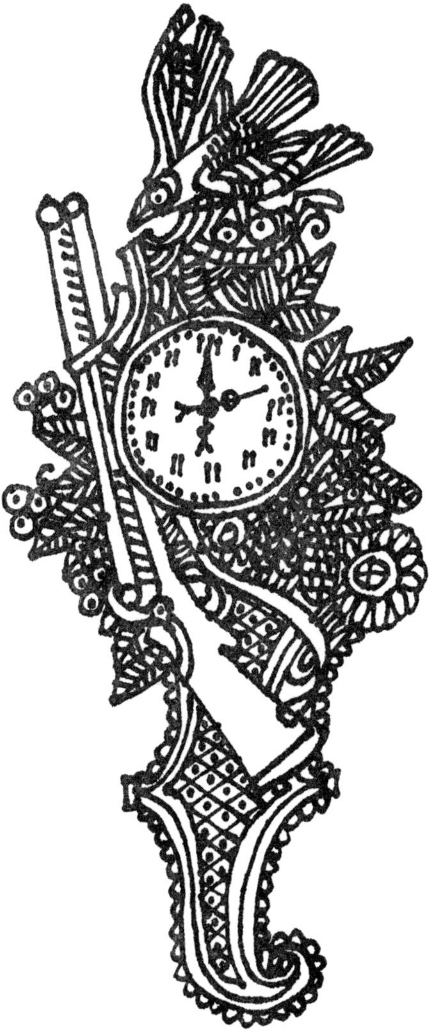

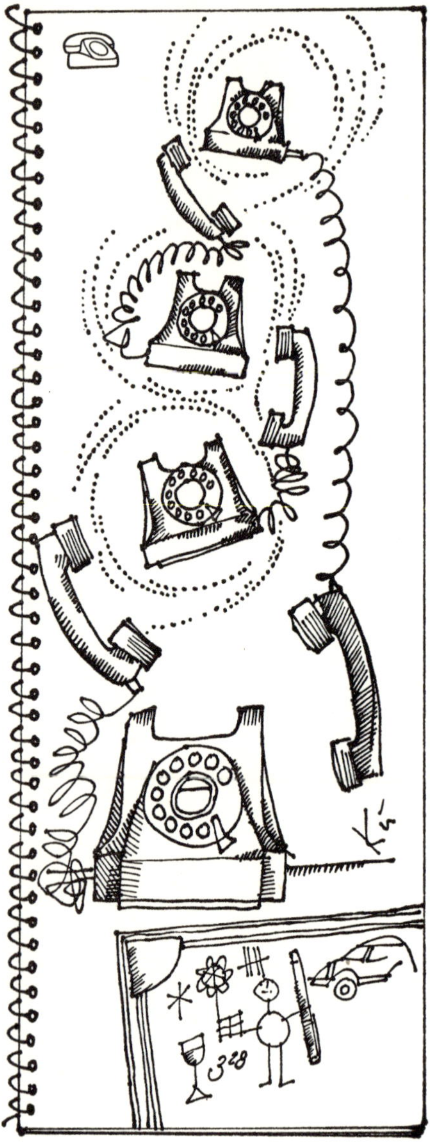

Hard Work

"Condungeonthorp Associates ... good morning. Who's calling, please?"

"This is Mr. Epstein, of Eugene and Epstein, Inc. May I speak to Mr. Condungeonthorp, please?"

"I'm sorry, sir, he's in a meeting – an all-day meeting. May I help you?"

"Thank you, but it's personal. He's a friend of mine."

"I understand, sir. Could you possibly call back tomorrow?"

"No, I really can't. I'll be in London tomorrow."

"When will you be back?"

"Late Friday night. I could call again on Monday. How would that be?"

"Ooh, I'm afraid he has a meeting at nine o'clock – but if you try a bit earlier, perhaps you can reach him. Is it important?"

"Somewhat important, yes. Would you please tell him that I called."

"Certainly. Any other message?"

"No, thanks ... just that I called."

"Does he have your number?"

"Yes, he does."

"And could you spell your name for me, please?"

"My name is Epstein ... E-p-s-t-e-i-n."
"... e-i-n. Right. 'Bye now, and have a nice day."
"You, too. Goodbye."

The Following Monday
"Condungeonthorp Associates – may I help you?"
"Uh, this is Mr. Epstein. Is he in?"
"Yes, one moment please. Oh, he's still talking on the other line ... would you like to wait?"
"Yes, thank you, I'll wait."
"I'll put you through as soon as his line is free."
"Thank you."

A Few Moments Later
"Hello, Mr. Epstein, are you still there?"
"Yes, I am."
"I'm sorry, but it seems to be a long one this time. Perhaps we'd better call you back."
"That would be fine, but doesn't he have a meeting at nine o'clock? That's in ten minutes."
"Oh, gosh! Is it that late already? How time flies!"
"Perhaps I'd better call back later."
"Okay ... but I really can't promise ..."
"Oh, please! I won't hold you personally responsible."
"That's nice of you. By the way, how was London, Mr. Epstein?"

"Very busy. I mean, I was very busy. As a matter of fact, London was also very busy ... but I did have time for a few plays and concerts and a couple of good restaurants."
"That sounds like fun!"
"Yeah, it really was. By the way, are you new at Mr. Condungeonthorp's office?"
"Yes, couldn't you tell? I started just last Monday."
"Gee, that's about when I first spoke to you, isn't it?"
"I think so. Uh ... Monday or Tuesday."
"Well, fine, I'd better go now. Will you be calling me back?"
"Yes, I'll have Mr. Condungeonthorp call you as soon as his meeting is over."
"Thanks very much."
"Oh you're welcome. Goodbye now."
"'Bye."

Monday Afternoon
"Hello, Mr. Epstein? This is Vreni at Mr. Condungeonthorp's office."
"Who's calling, please?"
"Vreni, Mr. Condungeonthorp's secretary."
"Oh, sorry. I didn't recognize your name."
"Didn't I mention it last time?"
"No, I don't think so. Actually, you don't sound like you would be called Vreni."

"No? How does a Vreni sound?"

"No, I didn't mean that. I meant that Vreni sounds so Swiss and you sound so American ... I couldn't detect any accent at all."

"Well, thank you ... I spent a lot of time in the States. I really like it a lot there."

"No kidding? Where were you?"

"Oh gee, practically everywhere ... north to Washington, through California, Texas, Louisiana, over to Georgia, where we have Swiss friends, then down to Disney World in Orlando and up to New York, with just a short side trip to all six New England States ..."

"Wow! Sounds like you sure got around! That's more than I ever knew about the United States myself!"

"You must be joking!"

"No honestly! I come from a little town on Long Island. Sure, I've visited a lot of places ... I'm always amazed that the Swiss know so much about the States."

"Well, like I said, I like it there."

"Yeah, you done told it like it was!"

"Say, that's pretty good! By the way, Mr. Epstein, you aren't *the* Mr. Epstein who writes books, are you?"

"Yes I am ... at times."

"Oh I knew it all along!"

"I could have told you earlier if you had asked.

But listen – uh – Vreni, you called me this time ... I almost forgot."

"Yeah, just wanted to tell you that Mr. Condungeonthorp wasn't able to return your call this morning – he had an unexpected client. Right now, he's not yet back from lunch, and when he does get back he has to run out to Kloten to pick up Jimmy O'Ruark who's flying in especially from Dublin just to see him."

"You mean that he won't be able to call me until tomorrow?"

"Sorry, but that's what it looks like right now. Was it very important that you reach him today?"

"Well, yes and no. But not to worry, Vreni, we'll survive the onslaught somehow ... perhaps with fortitude and sheer courage! I'll try again in the morning."

Tuesday Morning
"Hi, Vreni, this is Mr. Epstein. Is he in?"

"Oh hi, Mr. Epstein. Just a moment ... I'll see if I can get through. I think he has a client right now ... but maybe I can catch him anyway."

"Thanks very much."

"You're welcome."

A Few Seconds Later
"Mr. Epstein, I'm so sorry ... I thought he was

in his office, but he seems to have stepped out for a moment ..."

"Uh, Vreni, is there no phone in there ... I mean, where he is?"

"Oh you *are* funny! No, for your information we only have a phone in the *ladies'* room! You still want to wait?"

"Will he be very long?"

"Mr. Epstein, how could I possibly know?"

"I just thought. Well, you can't say I haven't tried to talk to him, can you!"

"No, Mr. Epstein, you've been very understanding ..."

"Yeah, I know. But listen, Vreni, I would still like to speak to him ... you know what I mean?"

"Of course, I'll get him to call you back sometime today."

"Actually I'd prefer to talk to you ... but business comes before pleasure, right? Ha-ha-ha!"

"Right! You men, you're all alike ... thanks God!"

"Ever thought what you would do without us?"

"I can think of several things, and if you call back later I'm sure to think of a few more!"

"You mean, you'd like me to call back later?"

"Why not?"

"Okay, then. 'Bye."

"'Bye."

Still Later That Same Day
"Hi, Vreni, how're you doing?"
"Hi, Mr. Epstein ... just fine! How are you?"
"Also, thanks. Say, you don't have to call me Mr. Epstein, you know. Why don't you call me Eugene?"
"Right, Eugene. Did you – uh – want to speak to Mr. Condungeonthorp?"
"You certainly have bright ideas, Vreni! Yes, that would be a good idea. Is he in?"
"He has a visitor at the moment – Mr. Shapiro, who flew in from Tel Aviv just to see him – but I gave him your message. Didn't he call you back yet?"
"No, not yet ... but I'm sure he's been very busy lately!"
"Yes, very busy."
"In that case, I'll call back in the morning. Thanks, Vreni, for your trouble."
"Oh, no trouble at all! Nice talking to you ... Eugene."
"Nice talking to you too, Vreni."

Wednesday Morning
"Hello, Vreni, this is Eugene."
"Who?"
"Eugene ... is he in now?"
"Is who in now?"
"Mr. Condungeonthorp."

"You must have the wrong number!"
"Oh, so sorry."

Wednesday Morning (Two Minutes Later)
"Vreni, this is Eugene ... is he in?"
"This is Heidi. Who's calling, please?"
"This is Eugene ... Eugene Epstein. Could I please speak to Vreni ... I mean, could I please speak to Mr. Condungeonthorp?"
"I'm sorry, sir, he's in a meeting – an all-day meeting. Can I have him call you back – let's see – on Monday morning?"
"You mean, I can't reach him before Monday morning?"
"I'm afraid not – he's in Paris. But I'll have him call you when he returns. Oh, wait a minute! Monday's a holiday ... I almost forgot. How's Tuesday morning?"
"Fine ... that'll be fine."
"Does he have your number?"
"Yes he does. Uh, by the way, where's Vreni today?"
"Oh, she's around ... must have stepped out of the office for a moment. Can I give her a message?"
"I thought there was a telephone – er – in there."
"In where?"
"In the powder room."

"Are you kidding? Anyway, I'll have Mr. Condungeonthorp call you on Tuesday morning. Goodbye, Mr. Epstein."
"'Bye."

The Same Day (Late Afternoon)
"Vreni, is that you this time?"
"Yes, this is Vreni – oh Mr. Epstein ... Eugene!"
"I wanted to speak to you this morning. I was looking for somebody to commiserate with – and I guess you were out."
"Yeah, I had to run out for some coffee cream."
"Do you ever run out for anything else?"
"Like what?"
"Oh, let's say a ... for a drink?"
"Here and there ... yes."
"Would you like to sometime ...?"
"When?"
"Today at six?"
"Why not?"
"Okay, meet you in front of your building ... how's that?"
"Fine."
"What do you look like, Vreni? Or what will you be wearing?"
"Red coat, brown hair ... I'm not too tall ... a bit too round, though."
"Stop it! ... I'm sure you're ravishing!"

"You men!"

"I know, I know ... spare me the painful repetition! See you at six ... in exactly two hours and – let's see – four minutes. 'Bye."

"'Bye, Eugene."

Still the Same Day (One Hour Later)

"Is this you, Eugene?"

"Yes, hello Vreni ... something wrong?"

"No, not really. But I have a little problem. I was supposed to pick up some shoes at the shoemaker's, some bread at the baker's and some cheese at the cheeser's ... ha-ha. That's a joke – he-ha!"

"I wasn't sure. You forgot, though, to mention the olives from Oliver's. You mean, you can't make it tonight?"

"That's my problem. I'm terribly sorry to do this ... I was really looking forward to it and everything."

"Well, I'm sure we can do it another time."

"Of course we can. But listen, Eugene, while I've got you on the line, Mr. Condungeonthorp seems to be free now ..."

"He's ... *what?*"

Mr. Condungeonthorp Is Free!

"Eugene! Where have you been hiding out?"

"Well, Sam Condungeonthorp! And what the

devil have you been up to? ... I've been trying to reach you for a coon's age!"

"Listen, if I told you, you wouldn't believe me ... I swear it!"

"What do you mean, Sam?"

"I mean, this one is absolutely the craziest, sexiest, wildest, horniest broad I've met in a long time!"

"What *are* you talking about, Sam?"

"This girl I met ... didn't I tell you about her before? She's staying with me now. I tell you, man, seeing is believing! This one you gotta see! What are you doing tonight?"

"Nothing, actually, I had an appointment for a drink with Vreni, but she just cancelled."

"Who's Vreni?"

"Your new secretary."

"Really? Boy, you really move fast! But why Vreni? ... she's not that great ... wide-body jet, if you know what I mean ..."

"That's not why I asked her, Sam. I've been trying to reach you for ten years and she told me you were in all-day meetings, at Kloten, with unexpected clients ... and all the rest. So we began speaking to each other and she was really quite pleasant. I thought it would be nice to have a quick drink with her ... nothing more, really."

"Hey! I appreciate your telling me all those

things she said to you on the phone. I told her that I would be tied up until further notice. Then I gave her my special list of forty excuses ... to use when people ask for me."

"Forty excuses? I don't believe it!"

"Yeah, I call them my 'Executive Excuses' – and they're great! Nobody can reach me, but they still think I'm working my ass off! Makes a good impression!"

"But aren't you working your ass off ... in a sense?"

"Of course, you know I work like hell. But not this week. This week I thought I deserved a rest ... so I'm spending my time with Veronika, *danke schön*."

"*Bitte schön*. And do you consider that a rest?"

"Oh my God, no! She's anything but a rest, but one hell of a number, Eugene ... you gotta see her! Can you make it tonight?"

"I guess so. What time?"

"Come on over now ... I'll be working late anyway."

"You don't say! You poor fellow!"

"What did you say?"

"Oh, nothing. Uh, Sam ... I'll be over in an hour or so. By the way, could I have a copy of your executive excuses? ... I think I can use them!"

"Sure thing, friend! So come on over. Say, I almost forgot! You said you were trying to reach me for ten years or something? Anything special you wanted?"

"Yeah ... I wanted to ask you – uh, I wanted to ask ... now what the hell *did* I want? I honestly don't remember ... but maybe it'll come back to me by the time I get there. Say, Sam, is Vreni still there?"

"Yes, she is. You want to speak to her?"

"Yes, please."

"Wait a sec', I'll pass you over to her ..."

Twelve Seconds Later

"This is Vreni."

"Hello, this is Eugene again. Just wanted to wish you a nice evening."

"Oh thanks. Same to you, too!"

"'Bye, Vreni."

"'Bye."

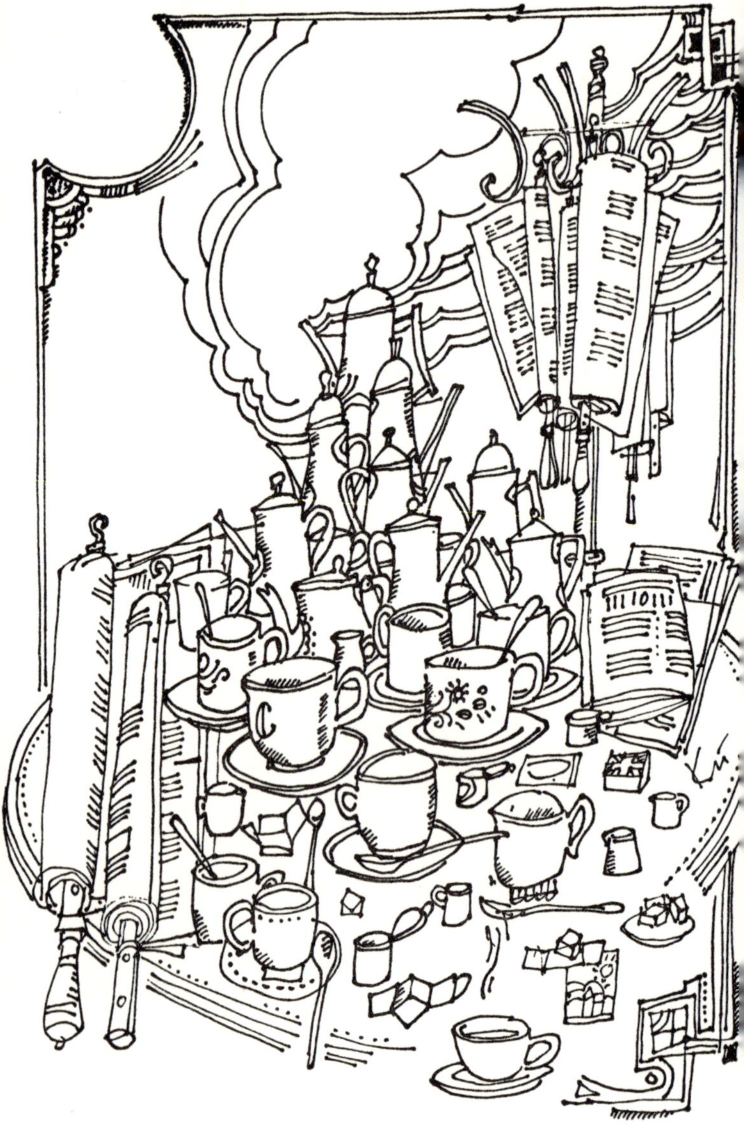

Beverage Leverage

Henry, an old friend from New York, arrived in Zurich a few days ago and phoned immediately from the airport. "Listen," he said. "I'm out of breath and suffering from jet lag and all that, but listen," he repeated. "I'm just dying to try that wonderful coffee bargain the Swiss have been advertising all over the United States!" "Coffee *what?*" I asked rather incredulously. "There's certainly lots of coffee in Switzerland, but I'm not so sure about the *bargain* part. Or were you possibly thinking of some other little country?" "No, damn it!" Henry interrupted. "Don't play games with me, Eugene. I've just flown in from Big Apple City for one single, solitary, specific reason: to have a one-dollar cup of coffee in Switzerland."

"Okay, okay," I replied patiently. "Tell us all about this theory of yours, Henry – I always thought that a dollar or more was quite a bit of money for a stupid cup of coffee." "Hell, no!" Henry continued. "Think of it! It may seem like a lot at first glance and first sip, you know, but I tell you, man, there's nothing like the value-to-price ratio for Swiss coffee in this whole magnificent world. In my opinion, the Swiss advertising genius who thought up the slogan 'Switzerland = 1 Dollar = 1 Cup of Coffee' ought to receive the Habsburg Cross, or whatever it is you people bestow on your national heroes. Just think of it! Coffee in America costs around forty or fifty cents, depending on the joint where you drink it, right?"

I wondered where Henry's fantasy was taking him. "Okay," he continued. "It's also usually somewhat lousy coffee, right? I mean, it quite often isn't really coffee at all, but more like a warm drink for the kiddies. Now – and get this, man – I discovered during my last trip to Zurich that, even though the dollar was worth 83% more than it is today, a Swiss cup of coffee is both twice as strong and twice as good, which more than equalizes the basic cost, right? Then, the Swiss give you at least twice as much time in which to drink your coffee, and added to this you can read two or three dollars' worth of newspapers and magazines and sit in a very pleasant café – not to mention the fact that Swiss waitresses are usually friendly and sometimes even attractive. Honestly, I'm so excited I don't know what to do! It amazes me that so few Americans know how inexpensive things can be in Switzerland! Just imagine, if I drink only 1800 cups of coffee during the next ten days, it will pay for the whole trip. And one other thing," Henry added as breathlessly as he had started. "In America you still have to add the tip!"

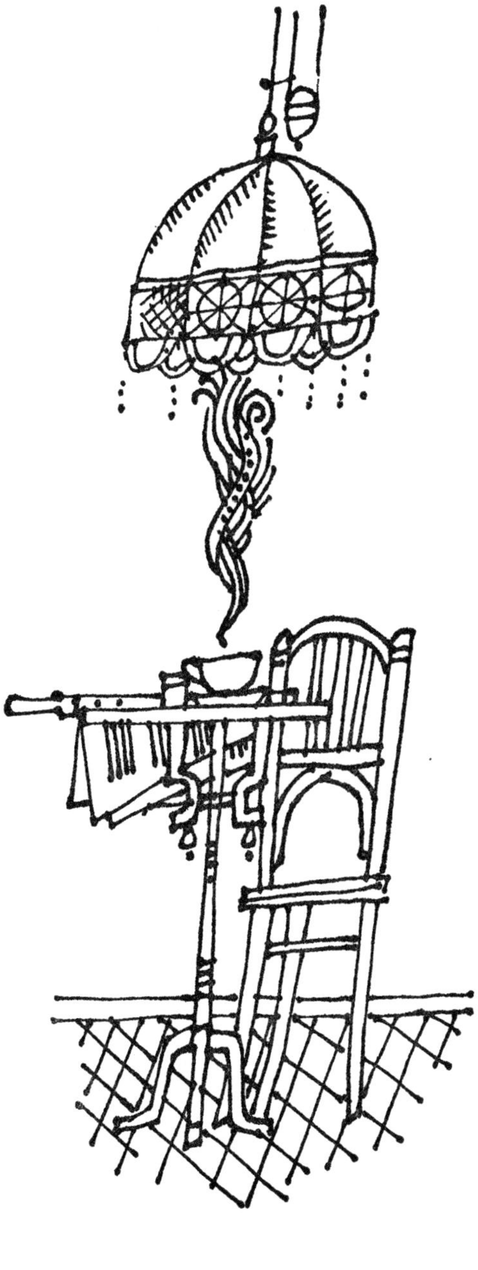

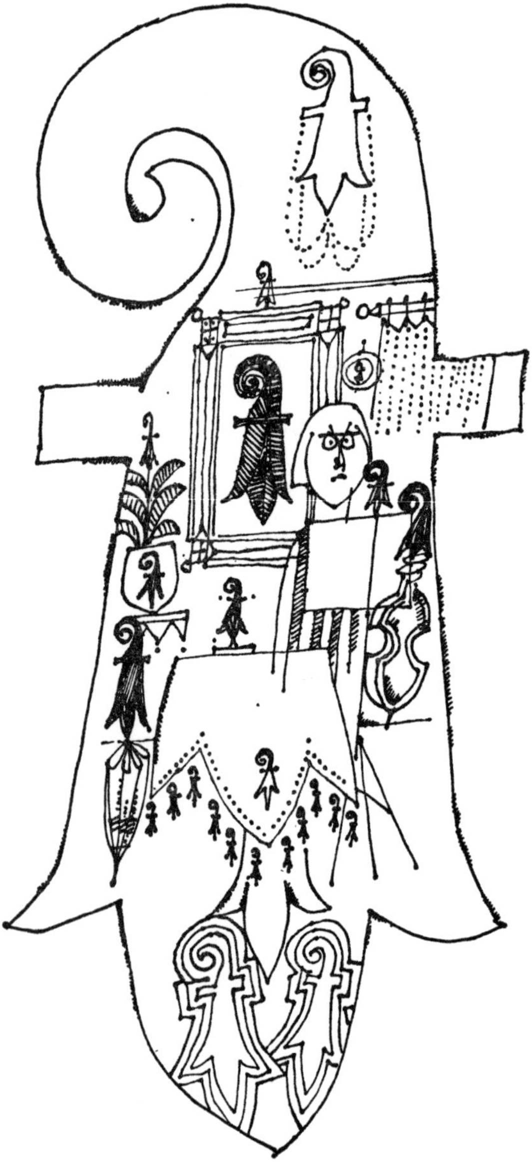

Dial L for Landlady

When I lived in Basel some years ago, it was a tradition among foreign students to meet regularly for lunch and to discuss the latest gossip over a steaming platter of spaghetti bolognese. Our group generally met either at the Lällekönig, a students' restaurant near the Rhine, or at the Spiegelhof, a café close to the university. Joe Kerr, an American friend of mine, was studying philosophy at Basel University, while I was at the Music Conservatory. One day at lunch, while pensively twirling an immense portion of spaghetti on his fork, Joe began to tell me about his landlady, Frau Annemarie Rotz. He described her as extremely cultured and well-educated, and he emphasized that she could speak six or seven languages fluently. According to Joe, who knew the Swiss far better than I, this was no mean trick, even in a country where everyone speaks at least three different languages. We spoke only one – and I'm not sure how fluent we were.

In any case, Joe thought it would be both interesting and edifying if I were to meet his linguistic landlady. And so it came about that I was invited, along with ten or twelve others, for a small glass of wine at Frau Rotz's boardinghouse on Aprikosenplatz.

It must have been an important occasion, for we were ushered into Frau Rotz's living-room, generally kept under lock and key. Like so many living-rooms of that era in Switzerland, it was used less for living than for displaying, and then only on Sundays and other similarly momentous occasions.

Joe introduced me to Frau Rotz with obvious expectancy. "Oh!" she asked. "How do you like living in Basel?"

Before a single microsecond had elapsed, she had answered her own question.

"Yes, I realize, Mr. Eggenstein, you couldn't know our lovely city *that* well yet and, anyway, there are so many *cultural* institutions here which probably don't interest you and ..."

I felt that I should reply to this incorrect assumption, but Frau Rotz was now gaining momentum and clearly had no intention of letting me interrupt the conversation.

"Of course you don't speak German, do you? And even if you did, you would still have to learn our very special dialect in order to grasp the many little nuances we Swiss constantly use when we engage in animalated dialogue with each other."

I didn't realize until now that Frau Rotz was speaking English – which is not that simple for a foreigner, is it? I was a bit embarrassed that I couldn't speak very much German – considering that I had already been in Switzerland for three-and-a-half months.

"Mr. – uh – what is your name again? Oh, I know – Epplestein. Mr. Epplestein, you know that we Baslers come from a very long line of ancestors – *patrician* ancestors – not peasants like those ignorant Zurichers! We have always had extraordinarily high cultural standards and a renowned interest in the Finer Things. Do you realize that almost everything important in this world was discovered, invented or developed by Baslers? Mathematics, medicine, education, philosophical thought – you know what I mean: Böcklin, Erasmus, Nietzsche, Holbein – all lived in Basel! My late husband, believe it or not, was the great-great-grandson of Professor Nasius Rotz, the famous mathematician and inventor of the self-winding abacus board."

I was most impressed.

"Oh, Mr. Hepplestein, have you already tried our wine? It's a very special white wine, you know – from the Rotz family vineyards in Weinheim in the Alsace ... just across the border and up a bit."

I had already emptied the first thimbleful – uh, glassful – which had been offered as we entered. In my opinion, it tasted like vinegar mixed with lemon juice.

"You see, Mr. Wettstein – oh, goodness, you know we even have a bridge over the Rhine with your name – any relation of yours? No? What a shame! Mr. Wettstein, do you know that there are houses in Basel that were already old, with their paint peeling and their roofs leaking, when Columbus first set out to look for your country?"

Now I was slowly beginning to get the idea. She was the subtle type. Okay, okay, I thought, I'll let her have it – with both barrels! But she still gave me no chance.

"Now Mr. Hemmingstein, you haven't answered my question – don't you consider that somewhat rude? I asked you earlier if you spoke German. Now I wonder if you even speak *English!* I mean, she added bitingly, *American* – naturally! Vast difference ... vast difference! And what about the *other* languages – important ones such as French, Italian and Spanish? I speak only five languages myself, which is very few for a person from Basel, but they do help me to get by in difficult situations. How many did you say you speak?"

I speaked. "Mrs. Rotz, I would much prefer to say something in one language than nothing in five!" I even *meant* it.

The unexpected silence was long, painful and pregnant. My remark came at one of those standard psychological lulls in the general conversation, when fourteen people suddenly have nothing to say and one person is heard all over the place.

That person was me. Uh, sorry – I. The change in Frau Rotz's demeanor was frightening. She was transformed from dreamboat to dragon in two seconds flat.

"Young man, such insolence! Considering your limited knowledge of European culture and breeding, I am astonished! On the other hand, I should have known – how could you *possibly* be different?"

Different? Yes, I am different, I thought. But it was precisely whatever breeding I had which prevented me from pursuing her further and moving in for the kill. While I was contemplating my next course of action, she relieved me of the problem by continuing her harangue.

"Typical Americans, all of you – I knew it all along. I have my nose full of you! Money, money, money! 'Time is money,' you say. The most famous American expression – ha-ha! – we all know it, don't we! And while you're out making money – or thinking about it – *we* are attending concerts, listening to good music by Ludwig van Beethoven, Willy Burkhard, Wolfgang Amadeus Mozart ... Hazy Osterwald. *We* read good books and go to the theater ... Johann

Wolfgang von Goethe, Shakespeare and the two Friedrichs: Dürrenmatt and Schiller. Oh what Titans!"

I honestly had no tights on, but how could I hope to prove it? I wanted to tell her that I, incidentally, was studying music in Basel but ... you know how these things go ...

"If you people spent more time with Mozart – ah, how divine! – instead of with Elvis Pressli – you would begin to understand what I'm driving at. Oh! It stinks me to even have to talk about it!"

Driving at? Driving me *crazy* – that's what she was doing! Blast it all! The others in the room – I was so embarrassed – they were absolutely frozen in their places, standing there like so many incredulous zombies. What should I say, what should I do? Was there no one present who might intercede and obliterate this unpleasant lady from my personal book of life? No. Apparently not. For God's sake! They – were – all – scared – to death – of – her! No one even moved!

And that's really all that happened on that particular day so long ago. But it's not quite the end of the story. Frau Rotz eventually quieted down, I quieted down, the other guests thawed out and the affair slowly came to its titillating end ... as affairs usually do.

"I so much enjoyed myself," said the hawk-faced harpie in the faded green dress as she limply shook Frau Rotz's outstretched hand. "It was lovely seeing you!" exclaimed the husband of the green dress.

"We must do it again sometime," suggested another woman. And all the other platitudes and clichés which commonly figure under the heading of conversation were likewise spoken and promptly forgotten.

"Screw you," I muttered quietly under my breath.

After leaving the festivities, Joe and I stood silently on the Wettstein Bridge (of all places!), savoring the chilly night air of Basel, transfixed by the river below. The Rhine spoke its own powerful and fluent language as it rolled relentlessly on to Germany and the North Sea. We listened to it talking for a long time before Joe broke the silence:

"Congratulations, Eugene! That was a great bit of repartee! In case you don't know French, it means that I'd love to have a bowl of spaghetti bolognese at the Lällekönig. Care to join me, monsieur?"

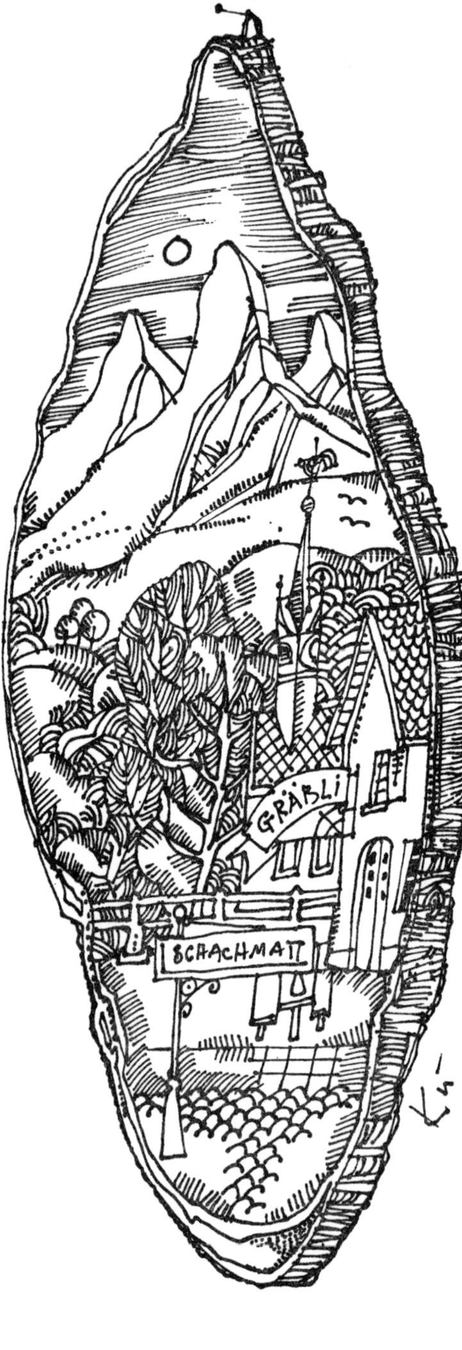

GRÄBLI
SCHACHMATT

Dialectics

Everyone knows by this time that illiteracy is virtually nonexistent in Switzerland. It is therefore not my intention to mitigate the importance of this revolutionary achievement, for there are precious few countries on the face of our adorable planet about which one could make the same statement.

After having lived in Switzerland for so many years – not to mention the months in between – I have had a unique Revelation. Revelations are generally unique, of course, but this particular revelation is crying out from within me: "Eugene, this is your unique Revelation speaking. Commit Me to paper immediately and share Me with the world!"

And this is what I did, for I had no other choice.

My Revelation and Subsequent Events
Imagine! I just realized why nearly every Swiss citizen can read and write! Why? Because there's nothing to read and nothing to write – at least not in Swiss-German. It's that simple! Should this fact not be peculiar enough for my readers, most of whom are noted for their extreme literacy, allow me to elaborate further.

There is, in any case, no earthly reason to write anything in Swiss-German, since there are few people who can read it or would even want to read it. What's worse is that no two Swiss can agree on how to spell in the first place, not to mention other fundamental sources of disagreement in Switzerland. The result is complete chaos, with people forever arguing with each other about how to spell – in their own language yet!

Take, for example, the word for "sausage", a poetic-sounding word which makes the heart of every Swiss miss a beat when he hears it. The word in German is *Wurst*. In Swiss it is *wùùrscht*. No one would argue with you about that – only the spelling remains so controversial an issue.

My friend Guillaume Gruyère, originally from the French part of Switzerland but now living in Zurich, was making a formidable attempt to learn Swiss-German. In order to do so, he foolishly thought he ought to read and write the language as well – not realizing that hardly a single publication ever appears in that language except during the Carnival season, when everything is *intended* to be funny.

So Guillaume – poor fellow – was understandably confused. Who wouldn't have been? "How we are to learn zee languages wizout zee books or zee paypers?" he asked me one day. What could I do but shrug my shoulders and offer him a sympathetic grin? Had I not experienced the same feeling of futility when I first arrived in Switzerland?

"Come, my dear friend," I said to him. "Come with me to a lovely country inn I know, where we can continue our inspired conversation aided and abetted by a hectoliter of wine or two."

So off we drove to a pleasant hostellerie, two hours away from my home, known as the Gasthaus zum Gräbli. It was located in the peaceful village of Schachmatt, at the foot of an awesome range of mountains, of which the Mutterhorn, Madhorn and Mudhorn were the most spectacular peaks. Guillaume was fascinated with the countryside. "Look!" he said, "a cow – *une vache* – *exactement* as we have in Fribourg, and zat's almost two hundred kilometers from here. Amazing, no?"

I was at the wheel of my trusty old Nickel-Daimler and had to concentrate on the road, so I perhaps missed the deeper significance of Guillaume's remark.

When we finally arrived at the Gasthaus zum Gräbli, I entered first – not because this is necessarily the polite thing to do in Switzerland, but simply because Guillaume would never have found his way through the billowing clouds of cigar smoke – and I had my boy-scout compass with me.

When we were seated, I asked Guillaume what

he would like to eat. "Guillaume, Tell me what you'd like. Shall we start with an appletizer?" His eyes popped as he craned his neck towards the neighboring table, where four hefty-looking and colorful gentlemen were playing *Jass*, the Swiss national card game.

"Oh, Eugène, look at zose sausages! Zey look beautiful! I will ordair two or three of them, *hein?* Do you wish to have Cervelats or Schübligs, Eugène?"

"They do serve a lot here, don't they!" I replied. "But I'm strictly a Schüblig man myself. I'll get the girl ..."

"No, Eugène, permit me ... I must practice my Swees-Jerman!" Then he raised his right hand and waved to the waitress.

"Fräulein," he said. "Wir möschten gärn a leetle beet of zat wùùrscht, bitte schön, eef you please."

Her reply was quite straightforward. "Wie-a bitte?", a question roughly equivalent to what they would say if a neutron bomb were dropped on the next village. In other words, she didn't understand Guillaume.

Then I tried. "Fröiläin ... bitte" (notice the nuance of difference, please) and so on until I got to the word for sausage, which I, of course, pronounced impeccably: wurscht. She seemed to comprehend this time, muttering something under her breath about two orders of "wirscht", but I have become accustomed to this sort of thing in Switzerland.

I asked Guillaume if he had understood what the girl had muttered under her breath. He replied that he hadn't been listening, as he was concentrating on the breath themselves. What a nut!

The sausages arrived – Schübligs or Schibligs or Schiblings or Schmucklings, all depending on where you come from – and they were hot, succulent and well-spiced.

"Succulent, aren't they!" I remarked. Guillaume almost died laughing. "Shall I reply to that one too?" he asked.

One of the card-playing gentlemen at the next table had noticed our predicament with the waitress and was listening in to our ensuing discussion concerning the language. It was Heiri Hodler, a local farmer, whom I had known for years at the Gräbli. We invited him over, waiting patiently until he had finished his Jass game and until he had unmistakably extinguished his cigar – fearing that it would extinguish us if he brought it with him.

"Grüezi mitenand!" he exclaimed – the friendly greeting one hears all over Switzerland (the spelling is arbitrary).

"Greetings, all together!" exclaimed Heiri.

"Would you like a cigar? They're the best *Stumpen* in Switzerland; made of aged compost – not like the others around here!" He introduced himself to Guillaume.

"Ah! Your foreigner friend here," he said to me. "Does he understand when we speak Swiss-German?" (This may look like a form of English, but may I ask the reader to use his imagination? The entire story would otherwise be rendered superfluous.)

"You may think it strange," I addressed Heiri. "But I'm the foreigner and he's the Swiss!"

He was dumbfounded. "You speak the language well," he said to me. "I don't recognize the dialect or some of the words you use, but I can tell that you're from somewhere in Switzerland. Your friend here speaks French. Is he from Western Switzerland?"

"Exactly right!" I replied. "He's from the Val Misère. And we're here tonight for the plain and simple reason that Monsieur Gruyère wants to learn the language. He's had enormous difficulty, however, mainly because you Swiss – I mean, *we* Swiss – don't believe in writing things down. Is this because of our notorious bank secrecy or what?"

"Herrgott!" our new friend screamed. "What in the name of Heidi's goat do you want to write in Swiss for? If you write it, somebody would have to read it. Which is impossible, because it can't be written. When we write – and we are people of very few words up here in the Helanca-Tal – we use *Schriftdeutsch*, or Written German."

"You mean 'High German', don't you?" asked Guillaume.

Heiri turned the color of the Pinot noir he was drinking. "Hochdeutsch, you say! Herrgott! That's what the Swabians speak!"

"Who are the Swabians?" Guillaume wanted to know. I came to the rescue. "Swabian is a pejorative term used in Switzerland to describe *all* the Germans, not only those who make their home in Schwaben. It is obvious that Heiri has no intention of reading and writing in *their* language."

"Then what's the difference?" Guillaume asked. "The difference," said Heiri, "is obvious. We read and write with a Swiss accent. How can you do that in High German?"

"Read and write with an *accent* – that's physically impossible!" Guillaume remarked.

"That's not true," Heiri replied. "Don't you ever watch Swiss Television ... or listen to the Swiss Radio ... or, well, just listen to all of us when we speak Written German?"

Guillaume looked confused. I could tell what he was thinking, but he chose to say it anyway.

"I am totally confused," he said. "First I learn in this strange place that you speak a language which you cannot write, then you write a language which you cannot speak. Am I correct so far?"

"Jawohl!" said the farmer. "Absolutely! What's so confusing about that?"

"Nothing, really," said Guillaume. "May I just take this subject one or two steps further? Logically speaking, the next step is that you read everything in German – not in Swiss – but you understand nothing of what you've read. Am I still correct? Then if you should ever decide to write Swiss, nobody will agree how the words they are written, because no one she knows the language he is speaking – nor the sounds they is making. Am I right?"

"I am not arguing with you, Monsieur Gruyère," said Heiri. "You are making all the noise around here. I hope you notice that we of the Helanca-Tal are people of few words – so it doesn't really matter, does it?"

"And all the newspapers," I finally added. "All the newspapers are in German, more or less the same German, with slight modifications, as spoken in Germany by the Swabians. These modifications are called Helveticisms, by the way, yet the German one reads is of a relatively high standard. How can you possibly explain this anomaly?"

"You call us animals?" cried Heiri. "What did I ever do to you?"

"Please, please, gentlemen, don't fight!" Guillaume interjected. "Eugène here was using one of his – how you say? – high-falutin' words."

"Janu," said Heiri. (No one knows what this word really means, but one hears it all the time.) "Janu," repeated Heiri. "What shall I do now? Can't you see that I'm going to cry? Look at me! My beautiful embroidered Swiss farmer's tunic (available in blue and red, 12% Poly, 78% Esther, 10% cloth, priced at fifty-eight francs) is already tear-stained. Don't you know what you are doing to me? First you come to the Gasthaus Gräbli (translation: Cleavage Inn) and mispronounce *wüürscht* so badly that I had an attack of heartburn on the spot ... it usually sets in only when I go to bed. Then you suggest that we can't read, can't write, can't speak ... Next you'll suggest that we can't think, either!"

"I was just coming to that one!" Guillaume admitted. "It's not thinking alone, but you'd have to admit that it has something to do with logic, right? I just want to know why you speak such a one-dimensional language ... as far as I am concerned, that's not what language is for. Look. Let's assume you're a farmer. If you own a cow and the cow goes 'moo', he wants something, no?"

"Maybe the moo-cow is in love with you," I suggested. "Did you ever think of that?"

"Quiet, Eugène. Let me continue. I merely wanted to say that a cow makes the 'moo', the baby it makes the crying, but neither cow nor baby must read or write to get what they want. Now what do you say to that, sir?"

Heiri shook his head impatiently. "Do you deny that Switzerland is a very civilized country?" he asked Guillaume. "Even if we should include the French and Italian parts? Do you deny that we have one of the highest standards of living in the world? If we have this – and we get what we want without reading and writing our own language – are we not perhaps better off than those countries *with* reading and writing? In other words, it doesn't seem to have helped them – you understand? Or do I have to give it to you in writing?"

It was now my turn. "Look, friends – Heiri, Guillaume – I think we're in basic agreement with each other. Guillaume is right in his way, Heiri in his. I was just wondering if it wouldn't be a good idea to standardize Swiss-German to the point where pronunciation and spelling would be consistent and generally understood. It doesn't make sense that you can't spell in your own language!"

"Sorry," said Heiri. "How can you spell if there

are two hundred and ninety-six different dialects with the pronunciation different everywhere you go? Why, just five kilometers from here, in Weiningen and Laughingen, they speak a language I cannot even understand!"

"*Mon dieu!* I think I'm going to be sick!" It was Guillaume. "Listen," he said. "In addition to not reading, not speaking and not writing – now you tell me you do not always understand your own mother-tongue ... This place is *incroyable!*"

"So what's so bad about that?" asked Heiri. "I just finished telling you that we're managing quite well, thank you, without anyone else's help – we Swiss. Why are you so worried?"

I continued where I had left off. "I am personally not so worried," I said. "I just wish that the spelling dilemma could be solved. Imagine if we had the same problem in the English language. Would everything look and sound like *The Canterbury Tales* ... or what?"

"I donut no wot ure tawking about," sed Heiry. "Purr-haps u plaice two mutch wait on setch non-cents. Franc-ly speeking, watts the difurents how u spel?"

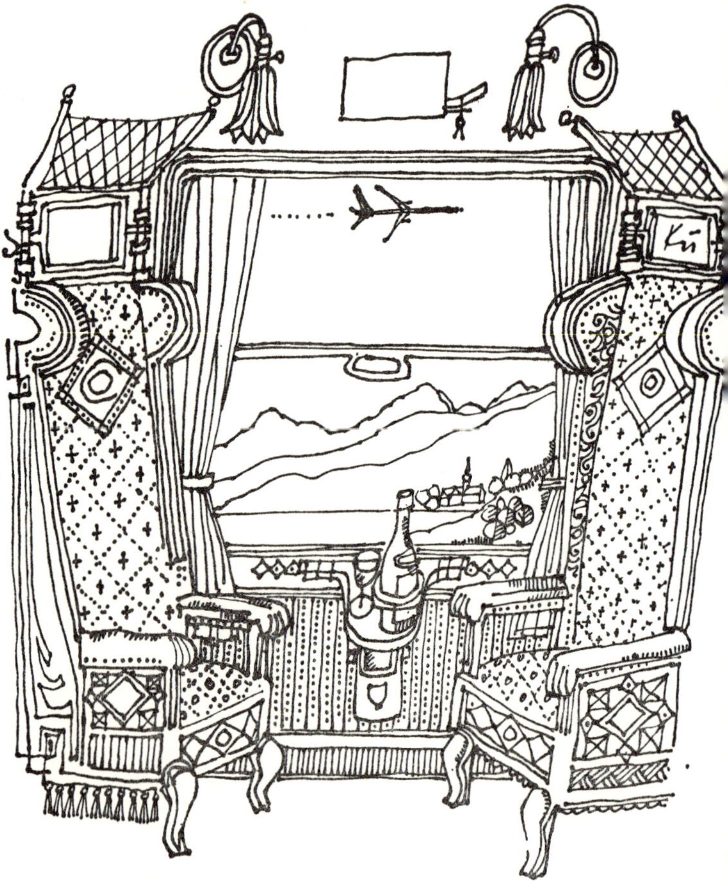

Choo-Choo Train

Railroads, despite their many attractions, have not yet managed to replace air travel as the most popular mode of transportation. Since many visitors to Switzerland – chiefly from the United States, where few trains exist – have had little opportunity to see or ride on railroad trains, we thought it opportune to describe, for their benefit, precisely what trains are and how they should be used. This writer, an American himself, still remembers that railroads – years ago – actually did exist in America, and he wistfully regrets that they are no longer in fashion.

Railroad trains differ from airplanes in that they generally remain on the ground. Because of friction and other such physical considerations (see A. Einstein: *Theory of Relativity*), trains do not move as rapidly as our modern jet aircraft, although they are occasionally faster than some small private planes and a good deal faster than the machine flown by the Wright brothers at Kitty Hawk.

Trains also differ greatly from aircraft in that they have no wings, which would obviously get in the way and would damage a lot of healthy trees. This would certainly not be in the best interests of our current environmental pursuits.

All railroads have one thing in common: rails. Without rails, railroads would by definition cease to exist and would soon become as odious to everyone as the automobile already has. Furthermore, without tracks, trains would not know where they were going.

In airline parlance, the driver of a plane is called a pilot. In railroad jargon, the driver is an engineer, a term possibly deriving from the fact that trains were originally drawn by steam engines – and the engineers were simply the engine-eers. At least that's my theory. They were not only the engine-eers, but the engine-eyes as well, for someone had to be responsible for the cars – or carriages – they pulled all over the place.

There are, of course, many other basic differences between train-riding and plane-riding and, for the edification of my readers, I shall describe those points of greatest interest:

Purchasing your ticket. When you undertake a journey in a Swiss train, you must first buy a ticket. But you need not reserve a seat except in special instances and for specific fast trains. Tickets are available in Switzerland at every railroad station in the country. There are several hundred such "stations", from reasonably small ones – in Herrliberg-Feldmeilen, for example – to the imposing, modern edifices of such cities as Berne and Zurich. In fact, to keep the record straight, there are more railroad stations in Switzerland than there are airports.

Boarding your train. Trains run according to fixed schedules, just as airplanes try to do. Unlike the airlines, however, railroads are less formal about when you arrive at the station. You can get on a train just four minutes before departure and nobody will care. The interesting thing about trains is that they have many more destinations than even the largest airlines. In Europe there are more than 100,000 miles of track leading everywhere you can possibly imagine. The trick is only to remember where it is you want to go, and then go.

The trains of Switzerland. This may sound like an advertisement, which I hope it does, because then I can call myself a copywriter rather than an author. Copywriters usually make more money than authors, and thus can afford to fly more often than authors. But authors are able to see more of the country from the trains they have to take. This helps to develop their powers of observation – which is why they are authors rather than copywriters.

The Swiss Federal Railways are known in Switzerland as the SBB (in German), CFF (in French) and FFS (in Italian). I would explain what these abbreviations mean, except that I'm not writing this to give language lessons.

What do I do on a train? Nothing. Just sit and gaze out at the idyllic countryside. If the countryside is not particularly idyllic at the moment you gaze, read a newspaper or strike up a conversation with one of your fellow travelers. There are no stewardesses on trains and no signs which light up with the admonition "Fasten seatbelts". In fact, there are no seatbelts, either. Now, if you do decide to ride the SBB, CFF or FFS (depending on the language you speak), and you end up enjoying yourself, why not recommend railroads to all your friends – especially those in the United States? The novelty might appeal to them. They may be puzzled at first, but they will certainly be pleased to learn that trains may now be added to the other common forms of transportation such as cars, buses, planes and skateboards.

The Swiss Slalom

Rainer Unsinn, who has just won the world skiing championship in the special slalom, is one of Switzerland's most popular sportsmen. It is not entirely unusual for the Swiss to be interested in skiing, but this year's champion has an unusual story to tell. Rainer Unsinn is a modest, well-dressed young man of twenty-two who grew up in the German-Swiss village of Bünzlikon in the Canton of Zurich. He is the first citizen of Bünzlikon to have won so significant a title, and for this reason we thought it would interest our readers to meet Switzerland's newest Alpine hero through this special interview:

Good morning, Mr. Unsinn. Thousands of people all over the world have been fascinated by your tremendous rise to international prominence in the slalom. To what do you owe your success?

"To the fact that I am – how you say? – simply faster than the others."

Yes, we realize that you are faster than the others, but could you perhaps explain to our readers *why* you are faster and how you became that way?

"Oh, excuse me. Of course, it is not enough that one is merely faster than the others, it is impor-

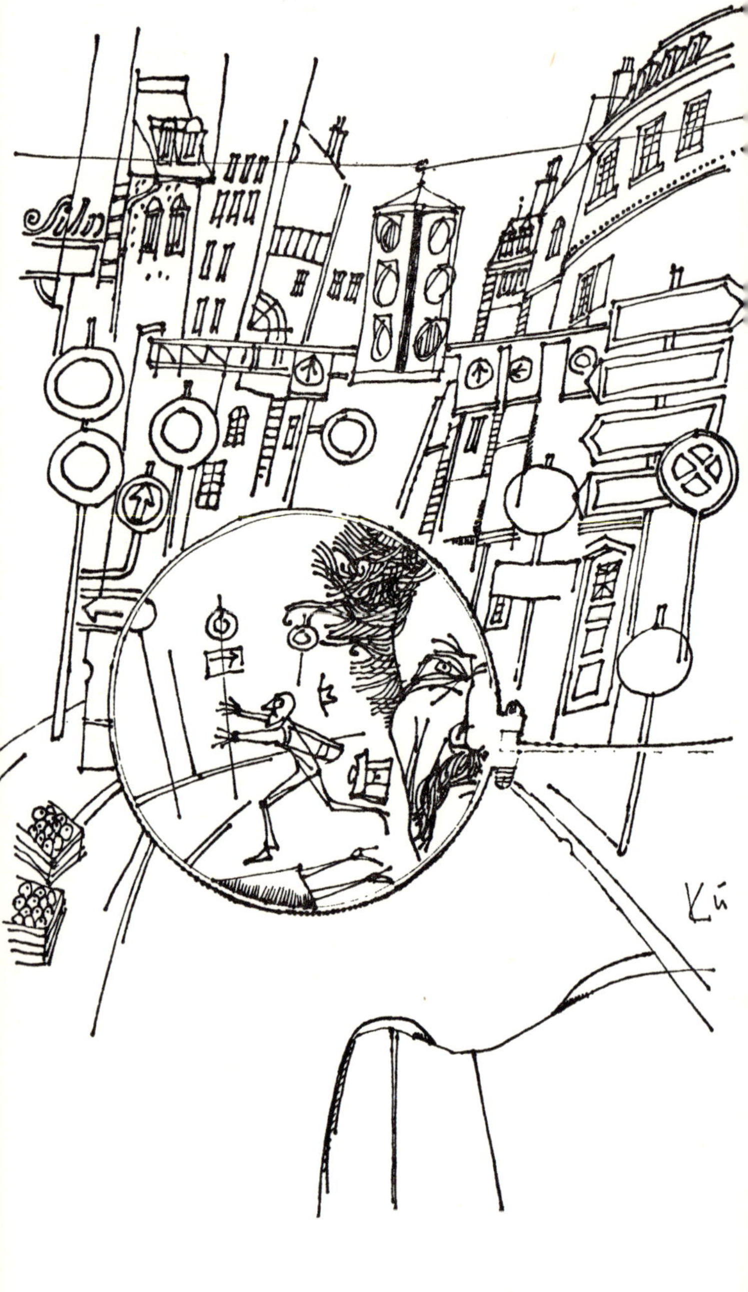
Kü

tant that the others are good enough to begin with, so that it then becomes worthwhile to be faster than they are. And, as you know, with all the many skiing contests going on all over the world, it is difficult to get enough good skiers together in one place to beat."

Yes, naturally. Well, we assume that you won your gold medal because of your unique and quite unorthodox style of passing through the gates in an amazingly rhythmical and fluid style. Could you perhaps comment on this?

"Of course, if you will please tell me what you mean by 'gates'."

Gates are where the flags are. You know, the red and blue flags you have to go through to win the slalom.

"Oh, why didn't you say so in the first place? I honestly never found out what those flags are supposed to mean. I just try to get down to the bottom of the hill as fast as possible, and those silly flags always seem to be in my way. My trainer, Freddie Blasmer, has told me over and over again to ski between the flags whenever possible. And this is what I do. It was difficult at first, because it's not easy for me to control my skis, especially when I have to turn left."

What, then, are some of the personal secrets of your trade? Why are you so much better than anyone else in the whole world?

"You know, I often wonder about that myself. After all, there are mountains everywhere – not always as picturesque and full of local color as those in Switzerland, but mountains nevertheless. And skiing, just between you and me, is not really that difficult. There's a lot of luck to it, you know what I mean? For example, you start racing downhill like a madman and sometimes you make it and sometimes you don't. That's part of the risk of this crazy business. Anyway, I decided some years ago that I would eventually become a slalom champion, because, as far as I could tell at the time, we never really seemed to excel in the slalom. So I practiced and practiced – summer and winter – and here I am, the world champion himself."

Excuse me, but where do you practice in the summer? In the Andes?

"No, actually not, we train mostly on the glacier above the Lac du Miroir, in Southern Switzerland, but I also practice right here in Zurich."

You mean you practice the slalom in Zurich – in the summer?

"Well, you see, I like to drive automobiles, too. I even thought once that I would become a racing driver, but I really don't like all that engine noise and exhaust. But I used to work for an insurance company in Zurich and had to drive to work every morning along the lake road. And this is really how I learned to master the slalom."

You learned the slalom while driving an automobile in Zurich? Could you please expand on this aspect a bit further?

"Surely. You probably know that there are magnificent pedestrian crosswalks in Zurich. I would even venture to say that they're among the best in the world, mainly because the yellow zebra stripes are always freshly painted – as is everything in Switzerland – and are thus visible for several hundred meters on a clear day. Zurich also has a lot of pedestrians. According to a study I personally conducted, approximately 42 % of Zurich's pedestrians are old ladies – and you know how old ladies cross the street! They simply do everything wrong: they look the wrong way, they hesitate, they move slowly – often with a cane or a crutch – not to mention that they are an absolute menace to traffic!"

Excuse me, Rainer Unsinn, but I think we're beginning to digress a bit. Our readers are primarily interested in how you developed your unique slalom technique.

"Just give me a chance, please. Well, while driving in to my idiotic insurance job every morning – especially on foggy days – my thoughts began to wander. I tried listening to the radio, but I soon grew tired of that as well. So I had nothing better to do than try to avoid Zurich's pedestrians, which is quite difficult, particularly since I like to drive fast, and, as you may know, it is not so easy to stop quickly. Gradually I developed a special technique – one I'm quite proud of – to avoid hitting pedestrians while nevertheless coming as close as possible to them. I guess I'm just rhythmical and musical by nature. When I see a pedestrian a hundred meters ahead, I let him think I'm slowing down. Then, just at the crucial moment, when he's in the middle of the street, I speed up again. If he steps forward, I pass him on the right. If he steps back, I swerve around to the left of him. But, in any case, I just manage to miss him, which, you see, is the same technique I use to pass those silly colored flags in the slalom."

Rainer, you seem to have some sort of deep-rooted hostility towards pedestrians. Why, if I may ask?

"What do you mean, hostility? If it weren't for pedestrians, we could raise the speed limit everywhere in Switzerland, especially in the cities. There will soon be more drivers than pedestrians, and I consider it completely undemocratic and un-Swiss to favor a minority when we, the slalom drivers of Switzerland, are not only in the majority, but obviously much stronger as well."

Returning for a minute to the slalom, Rainer

Unsinn, do you actually maintain that you became so good on the ski slopes because of your training as an automobile slalom driver on the streets of Zurich?

"Yes, I suppose so. In any case, I learned to avoid those childish blue and red flags on the *piste* just as I learned to avoid the old ladies of Zurich, all of whom know me by now. Perhaps it sounds somewhat sadistic, but I never once injured anyone with my car, at least not badly – and, between you and me, I don't intend to. Oh, I no doubt frightened two or three dozen old ladies during my insurance career. But I'm sure they would understand – bless their souls – if they knew that they were almost run down by the man who was to become Switzerland's first world champion in the special slalom."

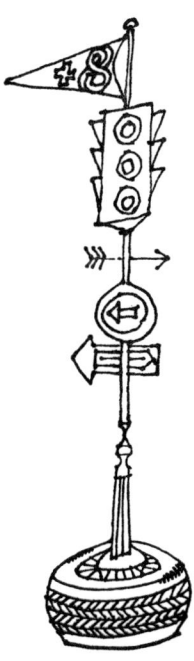

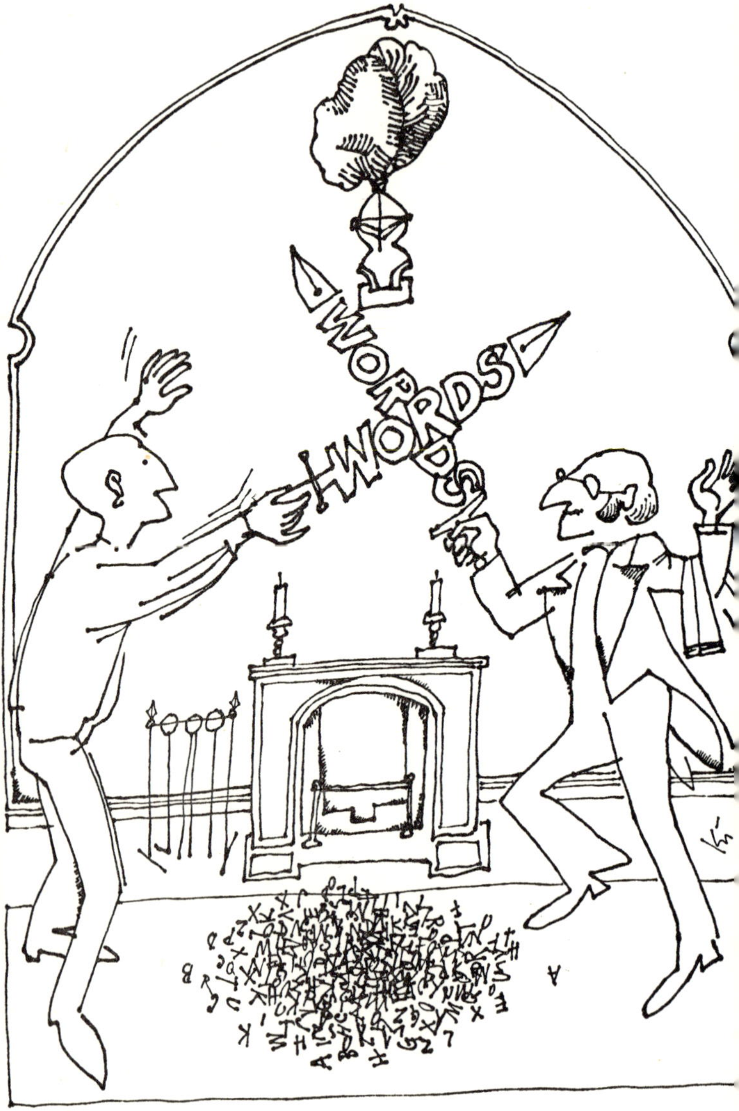
WORDS
WORDS

Mock My Words

In my opinion, it is important, *ab initio*, to speak foreign languages correctly ... from the beginning, one might say. But study requires time – not to mention effort – although not as much of either as, for example, an *affaire de cœur* or, in French, an *affaire d'amour*. However, being a staunch believer in *carpe diem*, I feel that using one's time correctly, strictly *entre nous* and *inter nos*, is just about *de rigueur*, if not obligatory.

Also obligatory in my life are the regular visits of Walti and Ruthli to my humble mansion on the Lake of Zurich. One day, while engrossed in the study of irregular Latin verbs, I was rudely interrupted by our butler, Stanhope, who wished to announce the arrival of two visitors.

"Begging your pardon, sir. As Madam is not yet up and about at this hour, I have taken the liberty of disturbing you in your private study."

"Quite all right, Stanhope, my good man – think nothing of it," I countered. "The 'Do not disturb' sign on the door is not an immutable law, you realize, but subject to interpretation and intelligent human evaluation."

"Sir, if you will pardon my persistence. I believe you told me yourself – last week it was – that rules and regulations in Switzerland are taken very seriously indeed!"

"Correct, Jeeves – er, Stanhope – absolutely correct. Except that my do-not-disturb sign was imported from New York City."

"You mean because it says 'Do not distoib'?"

"Right again, old boy! You do learn quickly, don't you? Anyone with half a sense of humor would realize immediately that the owner-importer of that there sign is not the sort of person who takes life so very seriously."

He winced distinctly. "Sir, begging your pardon again, but you recall my apprising you of the fact that humour is spelt with a 'u' – in fact, two 'u's' – not the rather ugly American way!"

"Stanhope, how could you possibly know that I said 'humour' without the second 'u' – this story hasn't been published yet. So let's not put the wagon before the dragon! Okay?"

"Sorry, sir, it was most inconsiderate of me, wasn't it! But I trust you will nevertheless remember that when you undertake the writing of said story, you will bear in mind that humour contains two 'u's'."

"Have no fear, my good man, have no fear! I may even allow myself a spot of levity in that I could theoretically ram the finished manuscript into your delicate esophagus. What would you say to that, my dear friend and butler?"

"Super, sir, simply super! But in your story you must switch to the third-person singular. For example, 'The writer rams his manuscript into the butler's windpipe.'"

"Stanhope, old bean, rams are *always he*-rams. So what we should really do is mix the rams with the 'u's' from before and let 'em loose with each other, right?"

"Yes, sir, very, very good, if I must say so myself! Ho-ho, very rich indeed! You mean the two rams and the two ewes ..."

"Yes, Stanhope, all under the unique title, 'Barnyard Sex'."

"I would prefer 'Group Sex', sir ..."

"Not *here* I hope, Stanhope! At least not today, please. I still have a lot of work to do – did you by any chance notice the little sign on my door?"

"Sir, forgive the intrusion, but I had originally intended to inform you that your visitors have arrived."

"They can wait a moment, Stanhope, especially since I'm not expecting any visitors – it's six o'clock in the morning!"

"Yes, sir. The title of your barnyard saga continues to confound me – if you will permit me to mention it again, sir. Perhaps the rams are merely wolves in sheep's clothing taking unfair advantage of two innocent ewes, who wanted nothing more than to have a brief romp on the verdant meadow. And don't you think, sir, that 'barnyard' might too easily be confused with the famous heart surgeon, Professor Barnyard?"

"Stanhope, you know what? I'm glad I hired you! Your humor – uh, I'm sorry, *humour* – is not as stilted as British humour is oftentimes reputed to be."

"Stilted? I do believe, sir, that Stilted is a cheese, is it not?"

"I ought to tear you limb from Limburger!"

"I have always adored limpy cheeseburgers – thank you very much, sir."

"Stanhope – my God, what a name! – Stanhope, will you please behave yourself! This conversation may have degenerated, but it nevertheless has nothing whatsoever to do with cheeseburgers, as every Hamburg burgher knows. Did you hear about the good burgher who went around saying, 'If I were king, if I were king ... I'd be a first-class burgher king!'"

"How puerile! I beg your pardon, sir, but if you will permit me to tell you of the marvellous cheese produced in a virtually inaccessible monastery in the Pyrenees ..."

"Ah yes, old boy! And very good cheeses they are, too! I have always had a particular fondness for holy cheeses."

"And back we are in Switzerland! Switzerland, land of holey cheeses!"

"Sir, as we can indubitably continue this edifying exchange of jocosity later in the day, I wish to announce once more that your visitors have arrived ... and are waiting."

"Who are they, Stanhope?"

"Walti and Ruthli – or so they have identified themselves."

"Holy Cheeses! I plumcake forgot! Stanhope, how many times have I told you not to digress? How many times?"

"Forty-two, sir."

"Stop being facetious ... how many times have I told you ..."

"Fourteen, sir."

"Bring them in, will you?"

"Yes, sir, right away, sir."

As I was saying before the interruption, it is terribly difficult to find help these days! Stanhope is clever, intelligent – good schools and all that tommyrot – but when I hire a butler, I am not hiring a *bon vivant*. I don't care what he knows. If anyone around here is going to be the *bon vivant*, I'll be the *bon vivant*, thank you and *basta!* And there's lots more to say on this subject but, at the moment, *je ne sais quoi ... je ne sais quoi*."

"Your friends, sir." It was Stanhope, politely ushering Walti and Ruthli into my private study. "Ruthli, darling! And Walti, schmuck! How are you two little devils, anyway? What are you doing up so early? It's only – uh – about six-thirty. Or has there been a total eclipse of the sun? What could account for such matutinal madness?"

They answered in chorus with the traditional "Grüezi Eugene" and got down to explaining their early presence at my posh lakeside villa.

"Eugene," Walti proposed, "why don't you come with us? We're on our way to Dirndlwald for a three-day course in advanced linguistics under Professor Konradin Kartoffel. The course is at the Three Kinks Hotel and includes, for four-hundred francs, pencils, paper and all meals ... with no extra charge for the indigestion."

I was slowly beginning to wonder what was going on this morning. Wait a minute, I mused. All I did was get out of bed, eat my modest breakfast of *jus d'orange*, young kippers and flash-in-the-pancakes, then ensconce myself in my study for a quiet three hours with irregular Latin conjugation. And what happens? All hell breaks loose – that's what happens! So now I obviously had to say something intelligent:

"Walti, Ruthli, please! I beg of you both! I am singularly honored that you thought of me, but I must unfortunately for the nonce ..."

"For the *what?*"

"Nonce, you dunce! As in *Non sequitur* and noncense ... get it?"

"Oh 'nonce' – why didn't you say so in the first place? Sorry to have bothered you, Eugene, but we both felt that your language could use a little polishing ... no offence intended, of course!"

"Of course not! That's what friends are for: to be honest with. Now why don't you and Ruthli – I love you both dearly and all that – now why don't you and Ruthli quietly get into your vaiting vehicle and depart for Dirndlwald by yourselves? If you would like a spot of breakfast before you leave, Stanhope will rustle up some grub for you."

"No thanks," said Walti. "Perhaps just a small *jus d'orange* ..."

"Stop showing off with your languages, Walti! Everybody knows that you're *non compost mentis* and, for that matter, not completely normal, either!"

"Non *compos* mentis, Eugene, won't you ever learn?"

"No, I guess not. I'm just an *enfant terrible*, a *rara avis* who just refuses to acknowledge that *tempus* always *fudges*. But before you go, and before you accuse me of another *lapsus linguae*, allow me one further *obiter dictum*. Or, as we Yankees say, another passing remark."

"You have been passing remarkably at my wife ever since you met her."

"That's right, kid! She's very hard to resist.

She's – how we say *en français?* – she's a *pièce de résistance!*"

"Thanks for the compliment," exclaimed Walti. "Nobody's ever called my wife a 'piece' before and lived to tell about it. Eugene, you're quite an exception, but one of these days I'll take you *al fresco* and beat your cerebellum into a you know what!"

"Walti, I would have considered such a remark to be completely *infra dignitatem* – in case you know what dignity is. However, it sounds like you're the guy who needs linguistics, so grab a glass of orange juice and ... *bon voyage*, okay?"

And so we parted friends, and, as has so often been the case, *en rapport*. More precisely, to use the comparative form, we parted *en rapaport*.

Well, *chacun à son goût* – no doubt about it! But I still don't understand why some people try so hard to impress others with fancy expressions. Does it give them *carte blanche* to go around confusing me, or do I always have to play the role of *bête noire?* This simply couldn't be *comme il faut*, could it? Oh well, back to business ... I still haven't worked on my *magnum opus* today. Wait a minute ... what about my *nom de plume?* I must ask Stanhope.

"Stanhope, would you come in a moment, please."

"Yes, sir?"

"Can you think of an appropriate *nom de plume* for me ... I need a pen-name right away."

"Sorry, sir, I'm not very good at naming pens. But if you'd like me to name your shoes sometime, please call again."

"One more *faux pas*, Mr. Great White Stanhope, and you've had it ... now go stand in a corner of the pantry for the rest of the day and leave me alone in my *sanctum sanctorum*. I am no longer interested in crossing swords with you. I am, how we Parisians say? ... *hors de concours*."

"But how could I have known that you were *ever* a streetwalker?"

"Oh darn it all! Get out of here once and for all, will you!"

"Yes, sir. Will there be anything else, sir?"

"Yes, Stanhope, as a matter of fact there is: you deserve a royal *potch* in your fat *tokhis!*"

Fin

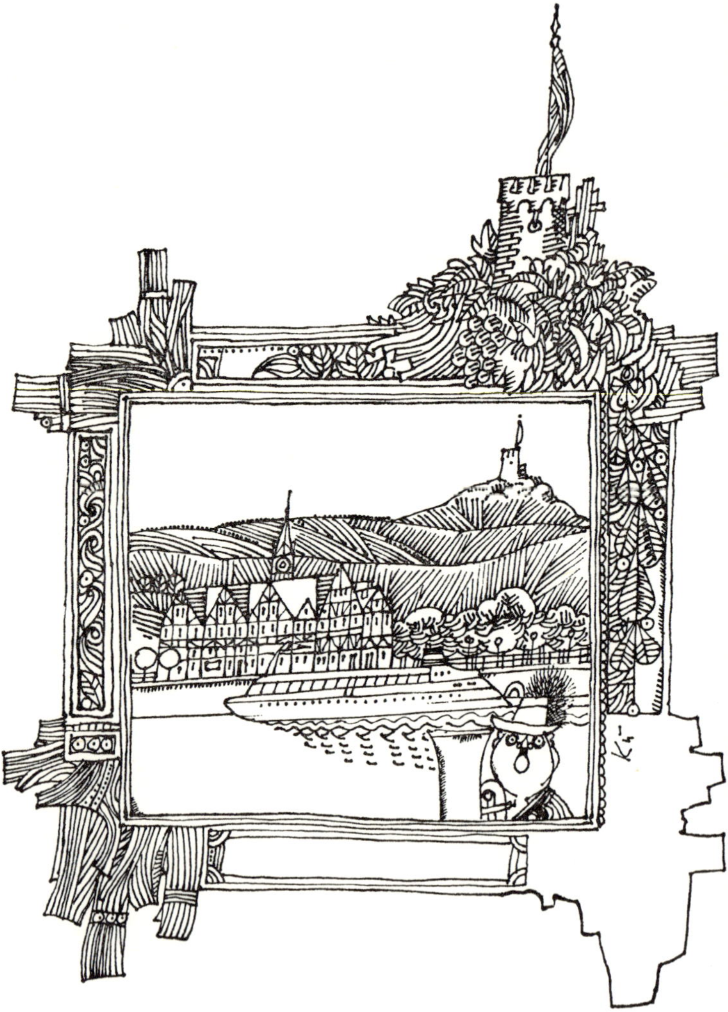

Life Can Be Fine

Warum ist es am Rhein so schön? This is one of the most important questions in Germany: "Why is it so nice on the Rhine?" The first thing to understand about the Germans and their undying love for the Father of Rivers is that the questions they pose seem to have more meaning than the answers they invent.

All right, then, why is it so nice on the Rhine? Any normal individual, travelling by boat from Bingen to Cologne, ought to be able to figure this out for himself. After all, there are lots of castles, hundreds of vineyards, and although the water itself isn't as pure and nice as it used to be, the river has always had a certain mysterious magnetism.

The Germans go for this mystery business. They love anything that has to do with the symbolic affairs of their Teutonic ancestors. Thus the Rhine takes on new meaning, with new words, most of them usually and neatly rhyming with the word Rhine. Anyway, why *is* it so nice on the Rhine? According to the Germans who sit around Rhenish winehouses until the early hours of the morning, it's so uncommonly nice there simply because "the girls are so gay" and "the boys are so thirsty". Now this is rather silly nonsense, one would have to admit, but our wine-drinking friends would never consider stopping at so elementary a point. The Rhine is so *schön*, they insist, because "the girls are so faithful" and "the boys are so free".

This last explanation is both curious and contradictory, for one can hardly imagine how in the name of Sieglinde all the girls can be faithful and all the boys free. I mean, who the devil are they free with, anyway?

To cap all this sophomoric symbolism, we now get yet another explanation from our Rhine poet, and you really can't argue too much with him: It's so *schön* on the Rhine this time because "one's blood is warm there" and "the wine is so good there".

This seems to be as acceptable a reason as any, certainly better than the ones about evil spirits haunting the castles and telling stories about the dark swirling Rhine waters which echo the majesty of Germany's past.

But what's wrong with a little romance? It's certainly better to hear about the majesty and purity of the Rhine years ago than to subject its waters to closer scrutiny today. The one thing I always liked about the Rhine and the lovely undulating hills rising up from the great stream was the feeling of poetic inspiration which always wells up inside me when I see them.

When I see the Rhine, I always want to compose

Rheinlieder – or Rhine songs – too. So it's not difficult to understand why so many people wrote so many songs about this most German of German institutions – if a stream can be called an institution (in German it can).

The wonderful thing about the Rhine is its name. The god or goddess who thought it up must have been a very clever *Nibelung*, or whatever he was. Because he thought of having the word "Rhine" rhyme with the word "wine" in quite a few languages. This is not my own discovery by any means, for every tourist who visits the Lorelei must have heard this one at least a hundred times. But it's true: *Rhein* rhymes with *Wein*, "Rhine" with "wine", *Rhin* with *vin*, *Ry* with *wy* (in Swiss – so help me!), and beyond this my philological knowledge fails me almost completely. However, I do know that in Nantitchi, a tongue spoken on the Outer Peninsula of Upper Wattabulli, the word for Rhine is "stachamanzu" while the word for wine is "watchacando" – another example of the universal appeal of this mighty river.

As I started to say, I like to write Rhine songs. I enjoy this splendid occupation because Rhine songs are so satisfying and because life can be summed up in a few terse but pregnant sentences.

On the Rhine I feel fine. I feel fine because of all

the sunshine (when it isn't raining). The sunshine makes the wine, which I drink on the Rhine in the sunshine – and then I continue to feel fine.

That is just one example of the hundreds of such ditties I have composed while sitting in an inebriated condition in picturesque inns along the Rhine.

The Germans, though, do not seem so terribly captivated by my lines. A German friend of mine told me that my *Rheinlieder* were too simple and that I was trying too hard to answer questions instead of asking them. What I was doing, he said, was *explaining* why it is so nice on the Rhine rather than *asking* why it is so nice on the Rhine. I remember how he referred with reverence to the words of Heinrich Heine and A. von Bergsattel, not to mention the poems of H. Brandt. The last-named gentleman wrote one of the most inspired questions ever to emerge from the Rhine country:

What do the Rhine wines bring us? Wine from
  the Rhine.
God gave it us to cheer us, so fill the glass
  with wine.
Cling, clang, golden wine, Father Rhine, you
  beautiful Rhine!

Now we know that the vines along the Rhine bring us the wine. And that's also fine. Especially since you can't have wine without sunshine (diabolically enough, "sunshine" rhymes with *Sonnenschein*), and I suppose that that's fine too.

In order to make an already long story shorter, I ought to mention here that most Rhine songs are rather repetitious, simply because there are so few ways of saying you feel fine when you're drinking wine along the Rhine in the blazing sunshine. But never underestimate the mind of the German poet! And remember that Germany has always been referred to as the "country of poets and thinkers".

One particular poet apparently couldn't get enough wine *along* the Rhine, and he decided it would be nice if the whole bloody Rhine were wine. And that would *really* be fine. Even if the sun wouldn't ever shine again. So he wrote:

"How often have I thought, kids, wouldn't it be nice if a magician came to me surprisingly one night. And if he held his magic wand over my head and said hocus-pocus, and so on. And one, two, three, I would become a lively fish, and could then swim anywhere in the Rhine."

This fellow goes on to write (and sing) that if the waters of the Rhine were only wine, then he would gladly consider becoming a fish. Now, mind you, he doesn't want to become a fish merely to drink the winey waters of the Rhine – that would be too obvious. He of course would enjoy drinking a few hectoliters of fine wine, but he points out in his song that he could drink all he wants and not have to pay a single red *pfennig*.

Aha! Now we're getting to the root of the matter. It's not that the Germans are stingy, parsimonious or mean. It's just that they feel that wine is goddess-given liquid sunshine which belongs to everyone, including the fishes. I'm not so sure how long a fish would live with all that alcohol in him (or her), but, as far as I know, no one has ever subjected this theory to more extensive ichthyological experimentation.

There's another song which has always fascinated me. It's called *Was ist Wein?* But unlike many other songs which only ask a question, this one answers it, and immediately. The full title of this delightful ditty is, "What is wine? Sunshine!" And there you have it – once again.

Considering the fact that Rhine wine is by definition nothing more than sunshine, it's hard to understand why so many Germans should find it necessary to seek their sunshine in other countries. After all, what does an Italian or Spanish vineyard have that a Rhenish vineyard cannot offer?

Can you imagine, for example, an Italian vintner extolling the sunshine in his Brunello di Montalcino 1966? As a matter of fact, our Italian has probably had more sunshine than he can stand, and *his* songs are more likely to conjure up thoughts of how nice it is to sit in the shade and do nothing.

And this, of course, is why the Germans talk and sing so incessantly about the sun. Between you and me, they really don't have that much sunshine, despite what they try to tell you. And, by the way, if wine is really bottled sunshine, I don't understand why some of them are so sour. But let's be fair: certain Rhine wines are very good – especially the good ones. And what's so bad about being happy on the Rhine? Or, as one other song has it, "Come, drink and laugh on the Rhine".

I think that would be fine, sometime.

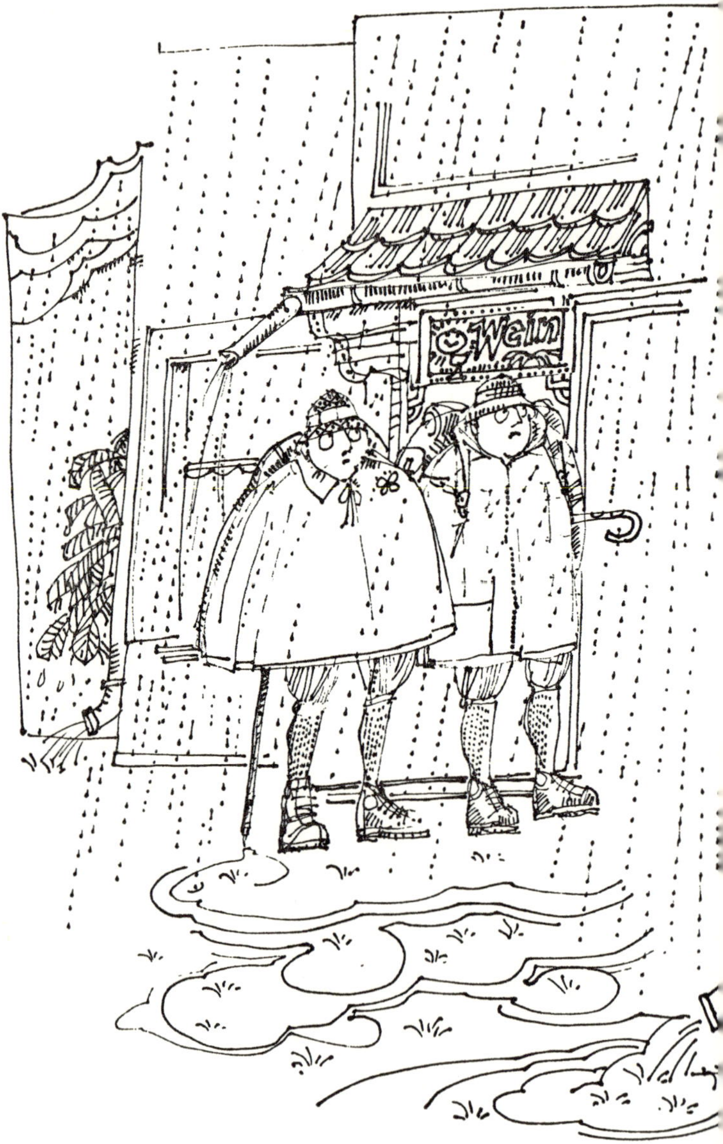
Wein

Talking of Walking

Eddie called one morning last week and invited me to go hiking with him.

"You came to the right friend, Eduardo my boy! I am the very personification of what you are seeking ... an experienced and highly trained ..."

"You never went hiking in your life, and you know it! Must you show off all the time?"

"How dare you make such an allegation!" I exclaimed. "As ridiculous as my suggesting that your name is not Eduardo!"

"It isn't, as a matter of fact. My name is Eddie ... remember?"

"As in 'Dirty Eddie', one of my favorite books?"

"No, Eugene, as in 'Eddie Is Ready'. And how about you – are you ready, able and willing to join us?"

"You know I'm not the joiner-type, but I shall make an exception for you. Tell me, though, Eduardo, do you think you can keep up with me on an extended trek? I'm in top condition these days – as you can see for yourself – while you have had a relatively active social life lately."

"Stop with your 'trek', will you? We are planning to go for a leisurely all-day walk in the Zurich Oberland. That is, if the weather holds up."

"Ah! The Oberland – an excellent choice, Eddie

– I'll be with you in the split of a second. The Zurich Oberland is rather far out, but why not? It's as good a place as any in Gorgeous Switzerland. We'll need about three hours to get there ... is that about right?"

"The Zurich Oberland, Eugene, is just over the hill from where you have personally lived for the past I-don't-know-how-many years of your life. We shall be going to the Bachtel, one of the higher hills in the area – about 1115 meters above sea level – which has a marvellous view of Eastern Switzerland."

"What do you mean *about* 1115 meters above sea level? Eduardo, what is my little Swiss world coming to! Please, my good friend, allow me to forewarn you – and remember that forewarned is forescorned. If you cannot provide *all* the facts, then we need not engage in conversation. Here in Switzerland, sir, I have been awarded the honorary title of *Tüpflischiisser*. I have been told that this is roughly equivalent to a doctorate in advanced engineering from the Federal Institute of Technology."

"You mean the ETH, don't you?"

"The ETH is the name of the school in German. I always refer to my alma mater in English: the FIT."

"Eugene, you are also one hell of a *Schnöri!* In case you don't know the expression, it means that you talk a good deal more than most people and possibly even more than you should."

"Thank you."

"You're welcome, Now how about finally moving your irresistible *derrière* and getting ready?"

"What do I need to take along?" I asked.

"Just the usual things, Eugene. You know, good, solid walking shoes, a windbreaker, sweater, hat, sunglasses ..."

"And sandwiches with dill-pickle slices?"

"No, Eugene – no sandwiches and no pickle slices. There are lots of good restaurants in Switzerland."

"How about a handkerchief?"

"Of course you may take a handkerchief! You don't have to ask me everything – I'm not your mother, you know!"

"Then why are you ordering me around like a mother hen? Just because you're a colonel in the Swiss Army you think everybody is dying to be ordered around!"

"I'm not a colonel, you buffoon! Only a captain – but I can assure you that my shoes are always polished, my dagger shined and my epaulets buttoned. And let me tell you something else, Eugene V. Epaulet. Once you've been an officer in our army, you can do practically anything. No mountain is too high to climb, no enemy too fierce, no ..."

"On second thought, I'd better stay home today, Ed. I forgot an important appointment."

"What kind of appointment?"

"For a haircut. My barberette is expecting me."

"In the first place, Eugenio, it's not true. And in the second place, you haven't got any hair in the first place!"

"Listen to the pot calling the kettle black, will you?"

"Eugene, for the last time!" Eddie implored. "Get your things and meet me in the car. I shall wait exactly 180 seconds for you and not a single week longer, understand?"

"Yessir, General! I shall appear as soon as I've collected the necessary and pertinent paraphernalia."

Owing to the fact that I keep my things in an orderly, neat fashion, I was quickly able to locate the equipment needed for our excursion into the Zurich Oberland. Everything is always in its place – in my closet and in life itself, a reflection of the way one thinks as an authentic *Tüpflischiisser* in Switzerland. I must remember to find out what this word really means. The Swiss always smile so sweetly when I call myself a *Tüpflischiisser*. I do hope that I can continue to live up to their demanding standards. They are extremely decent people, I thought. Here I am, a poor immigrant to their country, and they have accepted me with open arms. Isn't this what Captain Eddie meant when he asked me to go hiking with him today? He obviously considers me his friend and a good friend of Switzerland as well. For hiking in this country means more than placing one foot in front of the other and moving ahead. As I was about to find out.

"Here I am, Captain," I said. "Ready for the attack and at your command, sir! Take me to your personal flagship!"

"You're looking at it, *Tschooli!* My car is the flagship of our family fleet."

"Let's be off and gone," I said. "I daresay we've both had enough of this idle repartee!"

"You daresay right," said Ed. "And we still have to pick up Fritz."

"Fritz who?" I asked him.

"Fritz Pommes, a colleague of mine from officers' school ... he's now an infantry major."

"So was I," I ventured.

"So were you what?" Eddie asked.

"A major nuisance in my infancy, until I grew into adolescence and adultery. Now I'm a big boy."

Eddie looked perturbed. But he kept himself and the family car under firm control until we reached Fritz Pommes' house. Eddie went in to call him. When he returned, he was alone. He explained that Fritz had burned his fingers while frying potatoes and wouldn't be able to come with us after all.

What a pity, I thought. I was much looking forward to the warm camaraderie experienced by those who have been in the army together. Eddie, Fritz and I had actually been in different armies together, but the basic idea was the same.

"Tell me a Swiss joke, Eugene." It was Eddie speaking.

Eugene answered. "I don't know any Swiss jokes, Eddie – are there any?"

"You've told me dozens in the past. What happened to them, Eugene?"

"Oh, those! They were Jewish jokes with the names changed."

"Come on, now! What about all those old Appenzell jokes?"

"Right you are, captain! One Appenzell coming up! How do you want it – on white or rye, mayonnaise or mustard?"

"You have a very wry and mustardy sense of humor, even without the bread, you know that?"

"I am a Yankee born and bred, and bread is the stuff of life."

"*Staff* of life," Eddie corrected me. "Perhaps, now, with the help of your staff, you will favor me with the Appenzell story you mentioned previously. *Oder?*"

"Okay, you win! When does an Appenzeller stand on the tips of his toes, stretch his arms high above his head and wiggle his fingers in the air?"

"I give up," said Eddie.

"When he's playing the piano."

"That's absolutely not funny, Genius. Appenzell jokes are always the same – always the same nonsense about how small the people are!"

"Absolutely right, Eddie. Like this one: you know how an Appenzeller commits suicide? By jumping off the edge of the rug. Ha-ha-hee-haw! Or do you prefer the more conservative Bernese humor, since that is where you hail from? Did you hear about the two Bernese who went walking one day? One of them stepped on a snail and his friend said to him, 'Couldn't you have been more careful? You didn't have to squash that poor little creature!' The first fellow replied: 'I couldn't help it, he overtook me from behind!'"

Eddie was in stitches. "Very good, Eugene, I like Bernese jokes so much better than the other types of Swiss jokes. We may be slow – but o-ho! Am I right?"

We were now approaching our destination. The Bachtel – all 1115 meters of her – was directly ahead, and I was looking forward to our communion with Nature. The weather seemed somewhat threatening as we pulled up in front of a local inn.

"We'll need some sustenance before we get going," Eddie said. "This is one of my favorite old inns – they've got everything, from air-dried beef to air-dried sausages."

"Excellent idea!" I said as we entered. We ordered a bottle of Schiterberger Himmelsleiterli, despite the name a pleasant light-red country wine, and two portions of *Bündnerfleisch* which, to the uninitiated, is air-dried beef. If I were a poet, I would surely write an ode to *Bündnerfleisch!* Sliced paper-thin and eaten with the fingers, accompanied by slices of dark bread and a draught of wine, it is heavenly. I wanted to order a second portion, but Eddie wouldn't allow such frivolity. He emphasized that we were here to hike – and hike we would, starting immediately. We paid, put on our windbreakers and walked to the car, amid the rumble of thunder and the patter of raindrops. A peaceful summer breeze had suddenly turned into a full-scale squall. From a light drizzle, the rain increased in intensity until the pebbled parking area in front of our inn was inundated.

"What do you think we should do now?" Eddie asked me.

"Well, between you, me and the Swiss Infantry, I would suggest we temporarily postpone our walk and order another portion of *Bündnerfleisch*."

Eddie was not the sort of person who easily deviated from previously made plans. But he also saw the futility of pursuing our plan on such a day and agreed to my suggestion.

"What a shame!" I remarked as we re-entered the inn and sat down at our old table. "I would have enjoyed hiking thirty or forty kilometers with you, Eddie. That little hill over there – the Bachtel – that molehill among the majestic Alps – I could have climbed that hill with one foot tied behind my back! What a shame that we couldn't have done it together!"

"The Bachtel is 1115 meters above sea level," Eddie reiterated. "It's not for children, you know. But we'll go another time – have no fear – and then we'll find out how good you really are. In the meantime, have another glass of wine."

"Thanks, friend, but, if I do, I won't be able to sea level anymore. And what about you? You're still on your first glass."

"Me? I'm happy just to sit here and think."

"And what are you thinking about?" I asked.

"Oh, various things," he replied. "Mostly, though, about that hill over there." And he looked out of the window towards the mountains.

"The Bachtel?" I asked.
"Yes, the Bachtel," he replied. "I'll bet you right now that it isn't a single centimeter higher than 1110 meters!"

What's in a Name?

There's nothing quite like relaxing in front of the fireplace with a good book. And that is what I was doing the other day when my son Mike, eating a blueberry yoghurt, entered the living-room. "What's that you're reading, Chief?" he asked. "The telephone book?"

"Stop calling me 'chief', will you? Haven't I told you repeatedly that you may only use 'chief' in public so that everyone will know what I represent to this happy family? So please show a modicum of respect towards your father. After all, I *am* your father, you know!"

"Really? Okay, I promise to show more respect in the future. But, no kidding, is that really the telephone book you're reading?"

"Yes, it is ... you know very well what the telephone book looks like!"

"Of course I do! But most of us use it for looking up numbers – that is, when you are not monopolizing it. Last week I had to look for it all over the house, and I only found it when I looked in the upstairs toilet. Gosh! I hope there are no pages missing!"

"Mike, stop the nonsense, will you? I am peacefully sitting here in front of the fire, and you always interrupt at the most exciting spots ..."

"In the *telephone* book?"

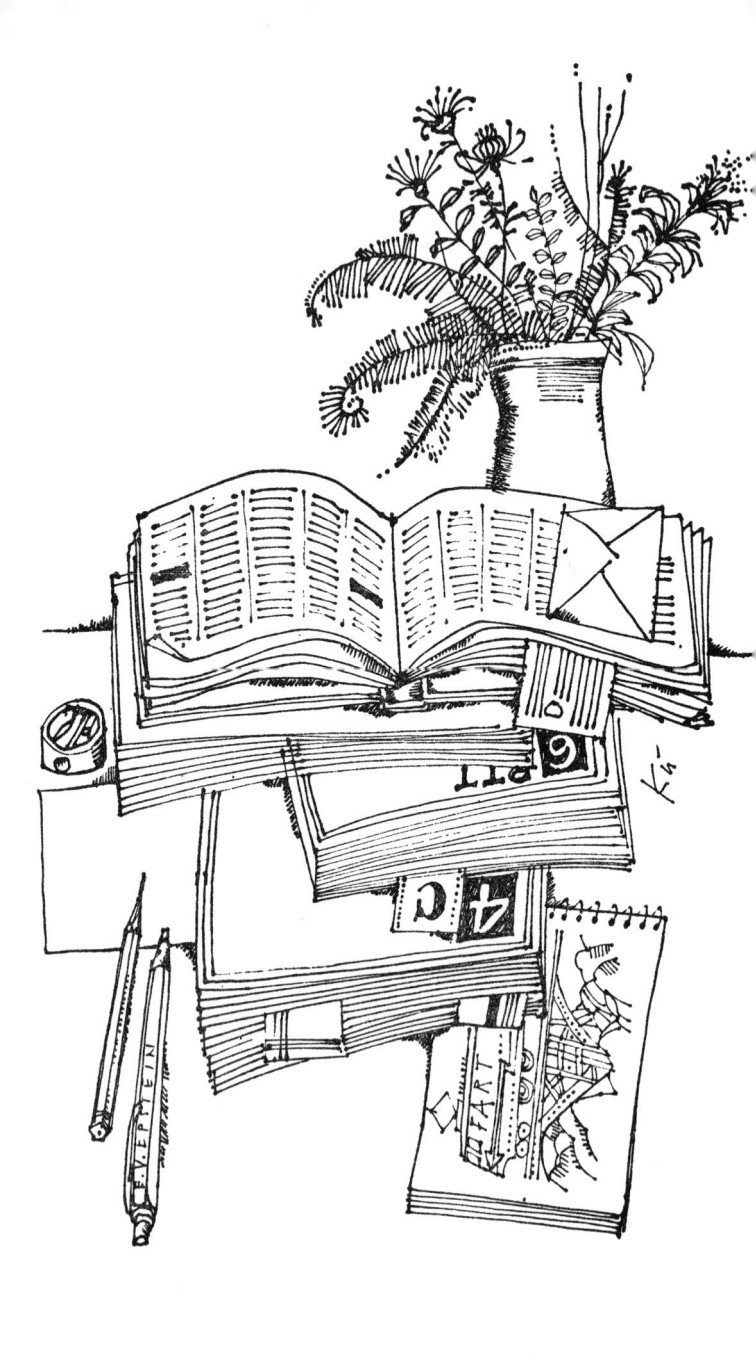

"Worse books have been written, you know."

"I didn't want to name them."

"Well!" I blared triumphantly. "That's exactly the point! You didn't want to name names. I'm reading a book that's *full* of names – thousands of names!"

"Are you feeling all right today, Dad? Or is there something I can bring you? A yoghurt perhaps – they're very good for the nerves."

"Will you get away from here with your infernal yoghurts, Mike! You're dripping blueberries on the carpet again!"

"How dare you talk to me like that, Chief? I never dripped blueberries on the carpet. Last time it was chocolate."

"And the time before?"

"Birchermüesli."

"Right. So will you please leave me alone now? Why don't you go upstairs and play Parcheesi with old yoghurt cups? In other words, my boy, I'm trying to concentrate."

He left and I was finally alone again with my book. The fire was crackling in, and warming the cockles of, my hearth, conveying a comfortable feeling of warmth and cheerfulness.

The fire hissed and sputtered as sharp tongues of flame began to scorch the bark of a piece of birch, a spectacle *en miniature* I have never grown tired of watching.

And I began reading further in the phone book. What's this? *Swissboring?* Quite possible – they sometimes are, I thought. But this is a company, in business to drill holes – like dentists. And who, I wonder, carefully studying the book, is Kunrat von Wurstemberger? What do people call him for short? With a name like Wurstemberger, he could be a butcher, or open a chain of fast-food restaurants. But who knows?

Not as interesting, I thought, as the next name I ran across in the book. *Mireille E. Saucy.* I swear it – and I myself am fairly adept at inventing names! I would like to meet Mireille E. Saucy sometime, if only to ask what the "E." stands for.

Or how about Barbara Glutz von Blotzheim, Gregorio Liberato Sablone or Remigius Spichtig? What sort of people are they? I'm so curious! And Haberthür V. Rumitas ... fascinating! I couldn't help thinking of an infant being shown to its proud and beaming parents for the first time. Mother looks at Father, they nod and collectively decide to name their first son Haberthür. And my son thinks that telephone books are for looking up numbers!

My imagination began to run wild as I thumbed through the other telephone books in the house, wondering what hidden treasures I would come across next. And while I was searching, I must have fallen asleep ... the fire was burning brightly and the atmosphere was so peaceful and cozy ...

Now I was sitting in a train, but I didn't know where it was going or coming from. If this was a dream, it was certainly realistic! The conductor was now asking for my ticket. "Where are you going – Domodossola?" he asked.

"I'm – I'm – I don't recall. What does it say on my ticket?"

"It says 'Domodossola' and I assume you bought it yourself. We'll be there in thirty-two minutes," he informed me. He punched my ticket and saluted smartly – at which point I noticed the brass letters on his conductor's hat: F-A-R-T.

"Forgive me for asking," I asked. "But why does it say FART on your hat?"

"We are in Ticino, sir, a sunny, southern canton of a country called Switzerland. And the acronym you refer to is the name of the railroad I proudly work for."

"The railroad? No kidding?"

"No kiddling! You are presently being transported between Locarno and Domodossola by the Ferrovie Autolinee Regionali Ticinesi, familiarly known, far and wide, as 'Fart'. What's so unusual about that?"

"Nothing, my good man. Nothing at all ... I was

just thinking ..." And I thought of other names and other places. Some years earlier, I had maintained a collection of various names and acronyms observed in Switzerland.

"Acronym ... acronym ... acro-bim-bam-bum ..." Somebody was tapping me on the shoulder. It was Mike. "Dad, you fell asleep ... and I need the telephone book. By the way, you kept mumbling one word over and over. What is an 'acronym'?"

'Acronym. Yeah – uh – that's a word formed from the initials of – well – several words of an organization or something like that. FART, for example, is an acronym."

"For what? French Art?"

"Oh, some Italian-Swiss name for a local railroad."

"Ah! Those Italians!" exclaimed Mike. "Imagine if we did the same with our railroads here in the north!"

"Well, actually, Haberthür, we *do* ..."

"Why did you call me habergrits just now?"

"Excuse me, I meant to say 'Mike'." And I began to tell my first and only son about the names I once collected.

"For example, I remember a similar conductor, with a similar hat, but he was in Arosa, and on *his* hat, in large brass letters, one could read the word LAW. I first thought that he might be a policeman, but he wasn't. LAW was also the name of a company – an aerial cableway called Luftseilbahn Arosa–Weisshorn."

"Is that also supposed to be funny?" Mike asked.

"I never said it was funny. It's *interesting*, that's all."

"Have you got more, or have we unfortunately reached the end of another exciting tale?"

"Many more, kid! Stick around for the continuation ... after this brief word from our sponsor: Me!"

I continued. "Mike," I said. "If you weren't such a SAP, you would join the MOB along with the rest of us PIPS."

"You're beginning to sound like some of the FAGS in the old city!" he replied.

"Ah! We're getting into the swing of this now! If it weren't for the generation GAP, we could go out on the town together. All you do is date the same old BAG all the time!"

"I what? I really represent that remark! How can you talk to me like that? When *you're* the guy who goes in for that S+M stuff!"

"I don't go in for S+M, you maniac! That's a firm in Zurich. In fact, there are two such outfits."

"Okay," he continued. "But you did tell me to meet you at the Schmuck Gallery last week, remember? And when I asked you why you were late, you said that you were delayed at the decorator's – I think the name was Pig Interiors. I'm really beginning to wonder if you're bringing me up correctly. I mean, is that the way to teach your children ...?"

"Children, my foot! You're not children, nor is your sister Deborah. So may I go on with the story?"

"Could I first have the telephone book? I want to look up something."

"What do you want to look up?"

"Hey! Wait a minute," Mike screamed. "Look at this – really rich! There are great names in this book!"

"That's what I've been trying to tell you for the last three hours ... what did you find?"

"I just noticed that there are a lot of very common names in Switzerland that have specific meanings in English ... like Wild and Hug and so on. Here's a woman named 'Rose'."

"What's so unusual about that?"

"She's named Rosa Rose ... that's why. And here's another one named Rösli Rose. Fantastic! Both of them married, too, so they married somebody with the same last name as their first names ..."

"All right, all right! I understand already! Anyway, as old Shakespeare said, '... a rose by any other name would smell ...'"

"A very rosy thought, father! And here are more: what do you think of Mary Bretzel, Molly Smart and Alice Wiggli?"

"Hey!" I replied. "Not bad. Let me have that book a second. Gosh, you weren't kidding! Allow me to introduce you to Helly Pigeon and – I swear it! – Rosy Talent ... Rosy Talent! Look for yourself!"

"Gee, Dad! There's one thing you can never take away from her: there's obviously more talent in her family than in ours."

"Speak for yourself, will you. Let's see now ... Regula Wolf ... just the way you act with the girls – you regula wolf, you! and ... uh ... Heidi Ho, who seems to be married to a Chinese. And what's this? Mike, how do you pronounce the name *von Euw* – E-u-w?"

"My God, Dad! Euw is 'Oy'. It's that simple!"

"Then why don't you tell me?"

"I just did. 'Oy'. You understand now?"

"Oy, do I understand! Von Euw is 'Oy'. Of course – what else? So be a good little boy, Mike, and go into the kitchen and bring your papa a nice cold yoghurt from the icebox."

"Sure, Chief, I'm on my way! What flavor do you want?"

"Blueberry," I replied. "It matches the color of our carpet!"

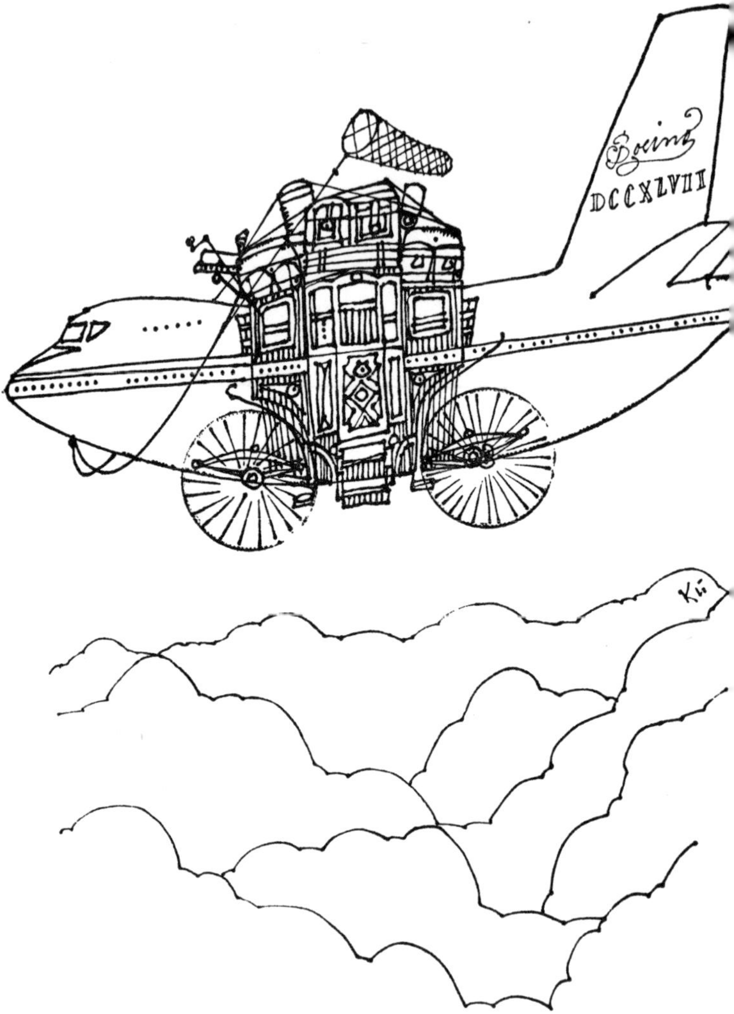
Boeing
DCCXLVII
Kü

Horse Sense

The Swiss are proud of their proverbial resistance to change. In other countries, change is encouraged, probably just to see what will happen – the philosophy being that things couldn't be much worse than they already are. In Switzerland, it's the other way around: there is an almost blind faith in the tried and true, while change itself is considered to be both uncertain and hazardous.

Perhaps this is why I respond so sympathetically to the Swiss and, of course, to their stunning country. For generations, things have remained as they are, because – and please ask any Swiss – it's usually "better" that way. And should you wish to question this approach to life, most self-respecting Swiss citizens will ask you to suggest a better place, and they might even ask you to catch the next diligence to that particular destination. This, for example, is what my friend Heiri thought I should do.

"Diligence? What's that?" I didn't understand the word and was forced to ask Heiri what he meant: "If you don't want me here, Heiri, I shall leave – as soon as I wipe away my tears. But please tell me first what a 'diligence' is."

"Typical, typical," Heiri replied. "You people from the Outside World move so fast that you no longer know what a diligence is. How ridiculous! Look here, Eugene ... look at this guidebook: my old, dependable Baedeker, containing everything you need to know about Switzerland ... if it's not in Baedeker, it obviously cannot exist! I insist that you use it constantly when you tour our Wonderful Country."

"That's fine, Heiri. But you still haven't told me ..."

"One moment, Eugene ... I'm trying to find the pertinent section for you. All right ... good ... here it is, clearly described in black and yellow."

"Black and ... what?"

"Eugene, don't you understand a Swiss joke when you hear one?"

"I'm not sure I ever heard one."

"'Yellow', Eugene, because this book has been in our family for generations and the pages have yellowed somewhat, that's all."

"The pages have yellowed somewhat ... the book has been in your family for ages ... and you suggest that I use it when I travel through Switzerland? Heiri, you're the doctor, but are you sure you know what ...?"

"Eugene, you're gemischt up again. I am a dentist, remember? My father and his father were the doctors in our family."

"Then who bought the book?"

"My grandfather inherited it."

"No kidding! Anyway, let me see it – I've never looked at an archaic Baedeker before – we can't have archaic and eat it too, can we? And it's in English! Didn't the German language exist at the time?"

"Come on now, Yank, it isn't *that* old, you know! The pages have turned such a pretty shade of yellow because my friends have used it so often. Imagine! This book has been all over Switzerland!"

"I'm most impressed, Heiri. Now where is the section you wanted to show me? I'm being very diligent."

"At the bottom of page ex-ex-ex-ay-ay-ay."

"I can see with my own ays ... uh, excuse me, aye-aye, sir! Heiri, what in the name of William Tell's chamber pot *are* you talking about?"

"Page numbers, Eugene! Page numbers in Roman numerals ..."

"Well! *Veni, vidi, vici,* Heiri! The book does look a little the worse for wear, but if the Romans used it, it must be good! Page ex-ex-ex-ay-ay-ay, you mean thirty-three, of course, and here it is!"

"Good boy! You see what I mean? If you always follow the instructions of your superiors, you are certain to get somewhere in life! Now read that page aloud to me."

I followed instructions. "The title is 'Diligences', and it reads:

"'*Diligences*. The Swiss coaching system is well organized. The diligences are generally well fitted up, the drivers and guards are respectable, and the fares moderate. The vehicles consist of the *coupé*, or first-class compartment in front, with 2–3 seats, the *intérieur*, or second-class compartment at the back, with 4–6 seats, which afford little or no view, and the *banquette* (used in summer only) for 2 passengers on the outside. In some cases there is only one outside-seat, which is reserved for the *conducteur*, or guard, but will be ceded by him on payment of the difference between the ordinary and the coupé fare. At the most important places, but not at all the intermediate stations, the traveller has a right to insist on transportation; and "Beiwagen", or supplementary carriages, are supplied when the diligence is full. When there are many passengers it is advisable to keep an eye on one's luggage, especially at a change of carriage ...!'"

"How beautiful!" Heiri said. "Isn't that simply beautiful, Eugene?"

"Yes it is, my friend. But with that vast mob of ten or eleven passengers, I would also be worried about my luggage ... you never know, these days ...!"

"So anyway, Eugene. You know all about diligences, right?"

"The word still sounds strange, Heiri. Unusual

word ... diligence. Where does it come from?"

"Diligence is from the French *carrosse de diligence*, or 'coach of speed'."

"Oh, I should have known! When did they use that expression ... in 1750?"

"No, Eugene, to be precise, about 1780 ... when your country was barely four years old. You see, we were already travelling around Switzerland in our speedy diligences ... just as you can today."

"Heiri, I hope you're not serious! How can I travel in a diligence today ... this is the second half of the twentieth century! America is more than two hundred years old ... there are no diligences today, Heiri, no 'Beiwagen' when the first one is sold out, no *banquette* and no *intérieur* for second-class passengers. Today's *intérieur* is called economy class ... and several hundred passengers can fly from New York to Switzerland in a Boeing 747."

"Seven-Four-Seven ... I'm afraid I don't understand, Eugene!"

"Excuse me, Heiri, I intended to say 'vee-ay-ay ... ay-vee ... vee-ay-ay', even though Alitalia didn't exist when Hannibal crossed the Alps."

"Are you pulling at my legs, Eugene? What are you talking about?"

"A Boeing 747, Heiri, is known as a Jumbo ... they fly all over the world carrying thousands of passengers everywhere ... every day ... to America ... Asia ... everywhere."

"Yes, but not into the Alps ... there are no jumbos in the Alps, Eugene. Not since Hannibal crossed the Alps with elephants to carry his luggage."

"Thank you for the history lesson, Heiri ... but how did we get onto this subject in the first place?"

"You said you wanted to take a diligence to the nearest foreign destination ... and I was only trying to help you out by showing you our family guidebook."

"But Heiri, be reasonable. You didn't really want me to take that book seriously, did you?"

"And why not?"

"Because it no longer reflects the true state of life in Pristine Switzerland! Look, this book must be at least ninety years old – if not more – and it just couldn't ..."

"And why not?"

"Because things tend to change, Heiri ... you know that!"

"They do not change ... they cannot change ... they never will change!"

"But they do, Heiri! Come on, friend, you can't be serious! Listen to what your book says on the following page:

"'The ordinary charge for a carriage with one

horse is 15–20 francs, with two horses 25–30 francs per day; the driver expects 10 per cent of the fare as a gratuity ...' You see what I mean, Heiri?"

"I know exactly what you mean. I always thought that 20 francs was too much – and for only one horse at that! Or did you mean that the gratuity is too high?"

"No, Heiri – none of that. I am not talking about one horse or two, nor am I splitting horsehairs regarding the tip ... I'm sure the drivers were entitled to every centime ..."

"Then what *are* you complaining about? Typical ... typical, isn't it! Every foreigner who comes to Beautiful Switzerland complains about high prices and forgets the quality we offer. Eugene, I've told you this so often!"

"Please listen for a moment, Heiri! I am *not* complaining! I am not comparing haircuts in Zurich to haircuts in Peoria – honestly I'm not. I'm not comparing hamburger prices or the cost of three ounces of popcorn, either. But I am trying to tell you, Heiri, that horses don't exist anymore ... do you understand?"

"Horses don't exist? All right, Eugene, horses don't exist. There are no horse races ... no horse shows ... no horse ..."

"Pssht! I'm trying to avoid using the vernacular, Heiri. Of course there are horses, but no carriages. In other words, the horseless carriage has been invented ... tra-la-tra-la! Let us rejoice!"

"I think you're beginning to go too far now," said Heiri. "Especially as there's nothing to pull your carriage."

"You'll go far, too, Heiri ... but I'd suggest you do it in an automobile."

"What a mixture! Automobile – Latin and Greek – how crude and oily. And why 'automobile', by the way? Does it drive itself?"

"Exactly!"

"... and what about the 10 per cent gratuity for the driver?"

"Okay, okay, cut it out! I shall assume for the remainder of this conversation that we finally understand each other. From this point on, Heiri, I shall talk to you under the assumption that you have heard of the twentieth century, that you know about the tremendous progress that has been made, not only in transportation, but in communications – just think of television, data processing ..."

"I don't like dates – much prefer figs myself."

"Heiri, haven't you looked around lately? Switzerland now has hundreds of miles of four-lane highways – fantastic engineering projects in themselves – with graceful bridges, with unbelievably long tunnels piercing the heart of the Alps almost everywhere! Heiri, it's no longer necessary to go *over* the Alps – even if you were to go in a diligence. Now you can go *through* the mountains, thus avoiding the snow, the glaciers, the avalanches and the St. Bernard dogs. Do you understand? We have made formidable progress in the last two hundred years, Heiri – since America was in diapers. Today we need less than an hour for a trip that used to take all day! Heiri ... Heiri ... that's what change is all about!"

He looked at me sternly. "What did you say?!"

"I said ... uh ... that's what – uh – change is ..."

"Enough now! How dare you suggest such science-friction nonsense? What have you been reading lately? H. G. Wells or Jules Verne?"

"Heiri, believe me ... it's true! Change can be marvellous, don't you think so, too? Come on, admit it!"

"Eugene, I have a few things I would like to say ... and a few questions as well. In the first place, I cannot believe this – how you say it? – this hogwash about four-lane hideaways everywhere ..."

"*High*-ways, Heiri," I interrupted.

"There couldn't be hundreds of miles of four-lane highbrows because we don't have the room in Switzerland for such experiments."

"They are not experiments ... they are fact! Why don't you go and look for yourself, Heiri?"

"Fact, you say! Then where did they put them,

these people who made them? Anyway, they would be washed away by this time ... all the snow and ice and water pouring down from the mountains ..."

"They are very sturdy roads ... made of the best concrete in the world."

"Eugene, for the last time, there are no roads like that in Switzerland! We do not need them ... not even for our very fast four-horse diligences. There is no room ... how many times do I have to say this to you? Where did they find the room? You don't think they would just go out and cut through people's homes and their property ... and no one would think of putting a road through our forests or our beautiful Alpine meadowland! No one! Which again proves that you don't know too much about us Swiss and our country."

"Heiri ... I can't stay here all day arguing with you ... I've got to leave soon. We'll continue the discussion next time we meet, okay?"

"Glad to, Eugene. But where are you rushing off to, anyway?"

"Oh, I was thinking about spending the weekend in Interlaken ... I know a nice waitress in one of the hotels!"

"Wonderful place! Wonderful place!" said Heiri. "A lot of English tourists, though. Stay at the Grand Hôtel et Beaurivage ... it's a bit expensive but well worth it because of the view."

"What do you think it will cost me, Heiri?"

"Well, they are a bit on the high side – but you could probably have a room with full board for about 15 francs."

"Heiri, forgive me ... but you can hardly buy a Bratwurst with Rösti for fifteen francs these days. Where do you get these weird ideas from?"

"From the guidebook."

"Pardon me – I *did* forget, didn't I! The guidebook ... how could I have been so stupid!"

"Exactly! Now listen, my boy ... it's really about time you got to know our Little Country. Let me read you something else from the book ... here, on page xvii."

"Couldn't you just say 'seventeen'? But go on, will you?"

"It clearly says that ... 'The cost of a tour in Switzerland depends upon the habits and tastes of the traveller. The pedestrian's daily expenditure, exclusive of guides, may be estimated at 12–15 francs, or even less, if he selects the more modest inns. The traveller, on the other hand, who prefers driving and riding to walking, who always goes to the best hotels, and never makes an ascent without a guide, must be prepared to spend at least twice the above sum ...'"

"I enjoy walking in Switzerland," I replied.

"But I plan to drive to Interlaken ... I have but a fleeting weekend at my disposal, you understand."

"Fine, Eugene. The diligence leaves at two-fifteen. I'm sure you can find space at this time of the year."

"Year? Which year, Heiri?"

The Last of the Wurst

The Lyoner sausage can best be described as resembling a heavy-caliber frankfurter in size, but closer to bologna sausage in flavor. For me, Lyoner is indisputably the king of salad sausages, despite the fact that Switzerland is literally swimming in a sea of sausages and similarly succulent specialties. The name "Lyoner" means that it originally must have come from Lyons, in France, or perhaps also that it is the favorite sausage of Lyons, not to mention Tygers.

Sausage salad – or *Wurstsalat* – may seem to be terribly commonplace and inconsequential to the Anglo-Saxon, but one should never look down one's nose at the simpler things of life. Remember that the world once scoffed at Auguste Escoffier, the creator of Escoffier coffee, and César Ritz, founder of the Swiss hotel dynasty, whose crackers are universally known for their superior crumbling properties.

In any case, my mouth waters when I think of *Wurstsalat*. *O lieber Gott!* If someone four miles away even whispers the word into the wind, I will surely hear it, with my stomach turning sympathetic cartwheels on the spot. My favorite *Wurstsalat* is prepared with a delicate mayonnaise dressing, to which a dash of Dijon mustard and various herbs have been added. At this

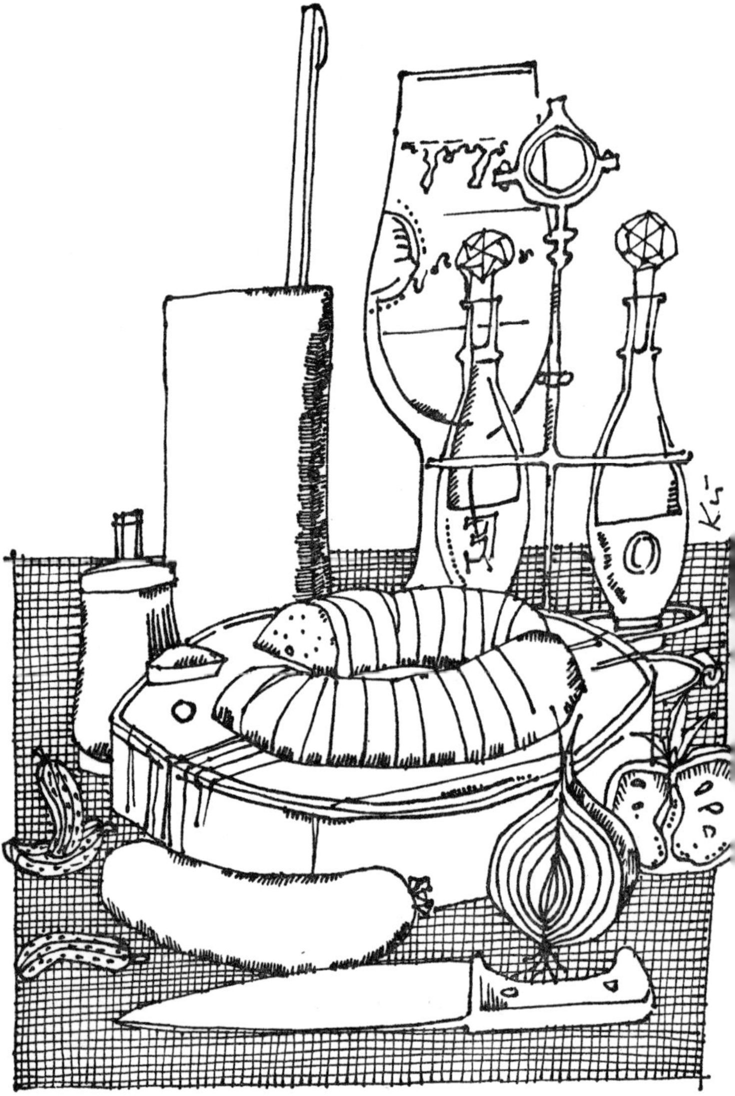

point, the sausage must be removed from its skin, even if the skin has not always been its very own. Then, depending on circumference and consistency, it is delicately cut into little cartwheels and lovingly placed, piece by piece, into the prepared dressing. Chopped Bermuda onions generally add a further subtle touch and bring out the full bouquet of this unique dish. The entire mess is then smashed around for a while and left to soak in its own juices. Should there be insufficient time for the marinating process, don't worry – the result cannot be worse. *Alors! Et bon appétit!*

The unsuspecting reader may begin to wonder what, in addition to the *Wurst*, has gotten into me. Perhaps this is why sausages are themselves so fascinating: one never really knows what's gotten into them. But that's a horse of a different color, if the *Wurst*-fanciers among my readers will forgive another unfortunate allusion. But why has *Wurstsalat* assumed so important a role in my life?

Years ago, while still a student in Basel, I discovered *Wurstsalat* at the same moment I discovered the particularly enchanting waitress who first served it to me.

Perhaps I discovered the girl first and was then embarrassed into ordering something, for I obviously couldn't sit and stare at her, could I?

I remember asking her, in English, what the house specialty was, and she rattled off a list of dishes as long as any I had heard in my life. Almost everything she said seemed to contain, or end with, the word "Wurst", so I ordered by mumbling something into my sleeve. The result, which soon appeared before me, was my providential introduction to nothing less than ... *Wurstsalat!* "*Wurstsalat spezial,*" the girl said as she placed an enormous portion in front of me.

That was my very first *Wurstsalat* – the first, I might add, of thousands I have subsequently consumed in Switzerland. I became a recognized connoisseur, for I ate *Wurstsalat* at the same restaurant every night of the week but Thursday, when my waitress was off duty. I always meant to find out her name, but I was quite shy in those days. But I did not intend to give up without a fight – I would someday find the necessary courage ... and would ask her name and where she lived.

Ha! Little did she know what evil thoughts may lurk in the hearts of men! How could she know that I was about to move in for the attack? I must do it now!

"What is your name?" I asked.

"With or without onions?" she replied.

"With onions," I groaned.

She hadn't unterstood me! Blast it! Why is life

so complicated? "Just you wait!" I muttered to myself. "I shall return!"

The following Wednesday evening I returned, and my waitress said something to me besides *Wurstsalat* and onions.

"Would you like a Bratwurst?" she asked.

Ah! Now we were making progress! Another three or four weeks and – who knows? – perhaps she would even tell me her name, provided that I asked her in a gentlemanly manner. In any case, my next course of action was clear. I had to act more self-assured, for girls don't respond properly to the insecure type of male.

The next evening I strutted into my restaurant like a peacock on the prowl. Sitting down at my table, I nonchalantly snapped, "The usual, please!" when the waitress appeared. That would impress her!

A few moments later, she placed a *Wurstsalat spezial* plus one grilled Bratwurst in front of me! She had caught me in my own trap! And the witch must have done it deliberately!

No! She wasn't a witch ... she was utterly wonderful! I wanted to take her in my arms and tell her of my undying love. "You're so *wonderful!*" I thought.

"I'm *what*, young man?" It was the beer-drinking lady at the next table. "What did you say to me?"

"Nothing," I protested. "Nothing at all – really not." She went back to her beer, and I regarded my cold *Wurstsalat* and warm Bratwurst, wondering what to do next.

When the Bratwurst had cooled, I surreptitiously sliced it into little cartwheels with my boyscout knife, dumping the pieces into my *Wurstsalat spezial*. My hopes of camouflaging the Bratwurst within the *Wurstsalat* were immediately dashed. For Bratwurst is white and *Wurstsalat* isn't.

When the waitress passed by the next time, an indescribable look of horror crossed her face. "What is *that*?" she cried. "Where did you get that *Wurstsalat* – from the competition down the street?"

I also wanted to tell her that I myself lived down the street and that I loved her. But the words, already formed in my mind and in my heart, nevertheless stuck in my throat.

Now I tried another approach, cleverly designed to appeal to her motherly instincts, which all women are supposed to have.

"You see, miss," I remarked timidly. "I'm all alone here in Basel, which you may have noticed during the past fourteen weeks, since I ate no less than eighty-four *Wurstsalats* ..."

"*Spezial*," she interrupted. "And you didn't eat eighty-four – only seventy-three, plus six Bratwursts – and that, for your information, makes a grand total of only seventy-nine!"

Oh, joy! We were actually talking with each other! We were engaging in mature human communication!

"Miss, what is your name, please?" I asked. Enough of this silliness, I thought, it's time to get to the point.

"That will be six francs forty-five. How many rolls did you have?"

"Miss, I asked you your name. I've been eating here regularly for months on end, patiently awaiting the opportunity to pop the question, and you persist in evading the issue."

"I'm sorry," she said. "I must have misunderstood. I don't recall your asking, but there's certainly no reason why you shouldn't know my name. I thought you were only interested in *Wurstsalat* and assumed that you were either giving me your order or asking for the bill."

"Yes ... yes ... I forgive you!" I cried. "But couldn't we someday ... I mean, rather sooner than later ... perhaps ... get together ... and ..."

She was gone again. The lady at the next table had finished her final beer of the evening and had called for the check. The waitress had disappeared into the kitchen, returning a few moments later with a sizzling platter of Wiener Schnitzel together with a veritable mountain of cauliflower and fried potatoes. Then she was suddenly on the other side of the room, serving Kirsch and wine to a group of ruddy-faced men who were playing cards.

When she returned to my table, I must have been day-dreaming. We were going to the movies together and holding hands in the balcony, walking through the zoo, doing all sorts of other things together. I awakened with a start from my reverie. She was talking to me!

"Six francs forty-five," she said. 'How many rolls did you have?"

"Two rolls ... and what's your name?"

"Sorry, but I can't talk to you now – I'm working alone tonight. Why don't you come back tomorrow? That will be six forty-five, please."

I returned the next day and the tomorrow after that as well, but I never found out her name. Nor did I ever have the courage to ask her again. But whenever I order a *Wurstsalat* in Switzerland, I am somehow compelled to think of her. Wherever she may be, I wonder if she knows that she once made an indelible impression on a young American student in Basel – a student who never paid for those last two rolls.